The High/Scope Educational Research Foundation is an independent, nonprofit organization with headquarters in Ypsilanti, Michigan. The Foundation's principal goal is to develop and disseminate practical alternatives to the traditional ways of educating children and training teachers. Program grants from both governmental and private sources support the Foundation's educational projects.

To further its goal of educational reform, the Foundation

- Has developed the Cognitively Oriented Curriculum for infancy through the early adolescent years.
- Operates demonstration classrooms for young children and a summer workshop for teenagers.
- Conducts professional conferences, workshops, and seminars for the training of workers in the field of education.
- Carries out evaluative research on educational programs.
- Operates a graduate-level training program in education and human development.
- Produces audio-visual materials for educators, parents, and others involved in the care and schooling of young children.

In 1962, Dr. David Weikart, then Director of Special Services for the Ypsilanti Public Schools and now President of the High/Scope Foundation, obtained local and state funds to operate a preschool program for children who, on the basis of local studies, seemed headed for failure. The preschool was located in Ypsilanti's Perry School. Federal funds later enabled extension of the Perry Preschool Project through 1967, and a total of 123 children participated (in either experimental or control groups) during the five years of its operation. Children in the preschool showed significant immediate gains on cognitive and aptitude measures, but more important has been the program's long-term educational impact. Longitudinal follow-up has shown that through fourth grade fewer than half as many children from the preschool program have been retained in grade or placed in costly special education classes than children from control groups (17% vs. 38%). To the best of our knowledge, the Perry Preschool Project's follow-up studies represent the longest continuous research in the country examining the effects of early education on the lives of economically disadvantaged children.

In 1968 Dr. Weikart was appointed Director of Research and Development for the Ypsilanti Public Schools and began four new projects: a demonstration and comparison of three preschool curriculum types, model sponsorships in the National Planned Variation Head Start and Follow Through projects, and a home-visit project for parents and infants—the Ypsilanti-Carnegie Infant Education Project, one of the nation's first experimental studies on the effectiveness of home teaching. In 1970 the High/Scope Educational Research Foundation was established to coordinate these and other projects in order to further the contribution of educational research to pedagogical practice and thereby enlarge the contribution of education to human welfare.

HIGH/SCOPE
EDUCATIONAL RESEARCH FOUNDATION
Ypsilanti, Michigan

Monographs of the
High/Scope Educational Research Foundation
Number Seven

YOUNG CHILDREN GROW UP:
The Effects of the Perry Preschool Program on Youths Through Age 15

L. J. Schweinhart and D. P. Weikart
High/Scope Educational Research Foundation
Center for the Study of
Public Policies for Young Children

with commentary by
Asa Hilliard
Georgia State University

Paul N. Ylvisaker
Harvard University

THE
HIGH/SCOPE
PRESS

Library of Congress Cataloging in Publication Data

Schweinhart, Lawrence J.
  Young children grow up.

  (Monographs of the High/Scope Educational
Research Foundation ; 7 ISSN 0149-242X)
    Bibliography: p.
    1. Perry Preschool Project.   2. Socially
handicapped children—Education—Michigan—
Ypsilanti.   3. Socially handicapped children—
Michigan—Ypsilanti—Psychology.   4. Students—
Michigan—Ypsilanti—Socioeconomic
status.   I. Weikart, David P., joint
author.   II. Title.   III. Series: High/Scope Educational
Research Foundation. Monographs of the High/Scope
Educational Research Foundation ; 7.
LC4092.M42S38   371.96'7   80-26061

ISBN 0-931114-08-X

Contents

Tables & Figures

Tables

Figures

Acknowledgments

This monograph builds on the work and cooperation of others. First and foremost, we owe our lasting gratitude to the children and parents of the Perry Preschool Project, nearly all of whom have completed interviews and tests, permitted access to records, and opened their lives to us over almost two decades. We are grateful to the Ypsilanti school system and other school systems in the area that have, with the consent of the parents, generously cooperated in providing us access to students and their records.

We thank Kenneth Polk of the University of Oregon for his contribution to the conceptualization of this monograph. His social-psychological approach to the causes of delinquent behavior became a useful framework for understanding the longitudinal effects of preschool education.

Charles Silverman, as editor for this monograph, played an invaluable role in its development from the very beginning. He has done as much as an editor can do to maximize the strengths and minimize the weaknesses in this piece of writing.

We are very grateful to reviewers of the draft version of this monograph: Nicholas Anastasiow of the University of Colorado; and, of the High/Scope Foundation staff, Terry Bond, John Clement, Elinor Jackson, Robert Halpern, and Bernard Banet. Their suggestions have unquestionably strengthened the writing that appears here.

We thank those who collected and processed the extensive data upon which this monograph is based. For the age 14 and 15 data collection, testers and interviewers included: Elinor Jackson, Gilbert Stiefel, Peter Bunton, Tony Cavallaro, Robert Dickens, Phyllis Dukes, Frances Laucka, and Paul Phillips. The data processing staff included Nancy Naylor, Jane Oden, Barbara Bruemmer, Jeffrey Moore, and others. Christine Tucker, Jeannette Melom, and Carolyn Nagusky provided assistance in assembling materials. In addition, present efforts could not have been made without the previous work of researchers, data collectors, data processors, and the teaching staff that operated the Perry Preschool program.

We wish to acknowledge the contribution of the High/Scope production staff, beginning with Pamela Woodruff who typed these pages. The text was typeset by Carolyn Ofiara and keylined by Dianne Kreis; graphics were prepared by Linda Eckel; production was coordinated by Gary Easter.

Financial support for this effort has been provided by the Ypsilanti school system from 1962 to 1970, the U. S. Office of Education from 1964 to 1968, the Spencer Foundation from 1971 to 1974, the Carnegie Corporation of New York from 1975 to 1979, the Education Commission of the States from 1977 to 1979, and the U. S. Bureau of Education for the Handicapped from 1979 to the present. The Carnegie Corporation also has provided core funding for the High/Scope Foundation's Center for the Study of Public Policies for Young Children, under whose auspices this work has been conducted. However, statements and views expressed here are solely those of the authors.

Finally, without the support of our own families, this work could not have been accomplished. It is to them that we dedicate this monograph.

Preface

The Perry Preschool Project is a longitudinal experiment designed to reveal the effects of early intervention on disadvantaged children. Begun in Ypsilanti, Michigan in 1962, the study compares an experimental group that received a daily preschool program (with weekly home visits) and a control group that received no intervention program.

This monograph reports the findings of the Perry Preschool Project from its beginning until subjects were 15 years old. In terms of the time span covered, it goes beyond two previous monographs reporting the study (Weikart, Deloria, Lawser, & Wiegerink, 1970; Weikart, Bond, & McNeil, 1978). At this writing the study continues, with data being collected from and about subjects at age 19.

The study was originally designed to test the straightforward hypothesis that early intervention has some positive effect on children. Almost two decades later, a more complex analysis is called for, partly because of the broad array of data to be examined and partly because of greater cautiousness among the public about programs which seek to alleviate the effects of poverty. Therefore findings are presented in terms of a set of interconnected pathways defining the effects of early intervention over time. The longitudinal study of early intervention requires the guidance of a conceptual framework. As the years go by and the data set grows in size and complexity, this conceptual framework is needed to determine the nature of data to be collected as well as aid in the interpretation of findings.

A truly longitudinal study is not likely to simply test a set of *a priori* hypotheses in the traditional scientific manner. The investigators, the scientific paradigms which guide them, and the cultural mood all change over time. Then too, the findings that appear during the early part of the study provide important feedback to shape the later part of the study, even to determine whether or not the study is to continue.

The Perry Preschool Project began as a local evaluation for a local audience. Now it is a pivotal study on the long-term effects, and even the value, of early educational intervention. Its audience is national and international. Fortunately, there have been several other longitudinal studies of early intervention programs. But the Perry Project appears to be the only longitudinal study of disadvantaged children meeting two basic criteria: (1) an experimental design, with experimental and control groups assigned on an essentially random basis, and (2) an early intervention program of daily preschool education and weekly home visits lasting at least one school year. As such, it is in a position to discover effects of early intervention in previously unexplored areas.

In the past decade, there has been a widespread belief that early educational intervention has not been effective in reducing the academic failure of disadvantaged children. This belief began with the negative finding of the first and only national evaluation of Project Head Start (Westinghouse Learning Corporation & Ohio University, 1969), despite the fact that this evaluation took place when programs were new and unseasoned. The belief was fueled by the reviews of Bronfenbrenner (1974) and White, Day, Freeman, Hantman, and

2

Messenger (1973). But the same studies reviewed by those authors have now revealed lasting effects of early intervention (Consortium for Longitudinal Studies, 1978). The Perry Preschool Project through age 15 not only presents evidence that early intervention can have lasting benefits; it allows us to organize these findings into a meaningful framework.

This monograph is written for everyone whose actions affect the lives of young children: parents, teachers, members of school boards, administrators, agency personnel, elected and appointed officials, legislators. If you are in one of these roles, your actions and decisions regarding children can now be based on an empirically supported belief in the lasting efficacy of high-quality early childhood education for disadvantaged children.

Lawrence J. Schweinhart
David P. Weikart
Ypsilanti, Michigan
June, 1980

"The most important thing you learn in a place is how hard to try."

I. A Framework for the Study of the Effects of Early Childhood Intervention

A chain of causes and effects is being traced in the Perry Preschool study to determine the nature of the impact of the Perry Preschool program on the lives of the children it served. The pattern, as we see it, is as follows. Preschool education provides children with a kind of cognitive interaction with their environment which they would not otherwise experience. As a result, they enter school with greater cognitive ability and, from the beginning, they do better in school. They know that their school achievement is greater; those around them know it as well. They are more committed to school and assume a role consistent with their greater school success. Teachers, parents, and peers acknowledge and reinforce this role, and it persists throughout their school careers. Eventually, they reap the rewards of greater commitment and success in school. They are less involved in school discipline problems and delinquent behavior. We predict that they will have higher educational attainment, find employment in higher-status jobs, and be more productive economically.

This explanatory framework for the pattern of effects of early childhood intervention is diagrammed in figure 1. Each arrow in the diagram points from a cause or category of causes to an effect or category of effects. "Cause" is meant in the scientific, statistical sense—a cause is not by itself sufficient to produce an effect, but simply makes the effect more likely to occur. These causes might as well have been called "contributing factors." This framework allows us to interpret the data on the Perry children's school careers through age 15.

The framework represents a *transactional approach* to the relationship between heredity and environment, between the individual and his or her field of operation. Both John Dewey and Jean Piaget espoused this position of ongoing interaction between internal and external factors in human behavior and development (Anastasiow, 1979). More recently, Sameroff (1979, Note 1) has focused on the temporal aspect of the interaction, proposing that the relative contributions of heredity and environment shift over time as well as differ from one aspect of behavior to another. The implications of this transactional approach to the issue of hereditary versus environmental influences are only beginning to be realized. Its applications to the design and analysis of empirical, longitudinal studies of human development, have been few (Field, Widmayer, Stringer, and Ignatoff, 1980; Werner, 1979, Note 2; Sigman & Parmelee, 1979, Note 3). We find that this transactional approach can provide us with a meaningful interpretation of the longitudinal data of the Perry Preschool study.

One area of application is the transactional interpretation of the development of cognitive ability. For many years, it was assumed that intelligence was almost solely determined by heredity. Then early childhood intervention studies demonstrated that cognitive ability could be improved, at least temporarily. The pendulum swung back as Jensen (1969) and others interpreted the return of IQs to their pre-intervention levels as an indication that cognitive ability could not really be altered. However, a transactional interpretation of the same sequence of events is that environments did contribute to cognitive ability: a stimulating preschool environment enhanced cognitive ability; a less stimulating elementary school environment, in the midst of conditions of poverty, depressed cognitive ability. Different environments influenced cognitive ability in different ways. * This way of thinking about the relationship between the environment and cognitive ability is central to our analysis.

---

* Some might object that this analysis was disproved by the mixed results of Project Follow Through (see articles in the *Harvard Educational Review*, 48 (2), 1978), since a basic rationale for this project was that special programs in elementary schools could maintain improvements in cognitive ability. But issues of implementation, differing objectives of various curriculum models, and assessment problems made a test of this simple hypothesis virtually impossible.

6

FIGURE 1 PROPOSED CAUSAL MODEL FOR EARLY INTERVENTION

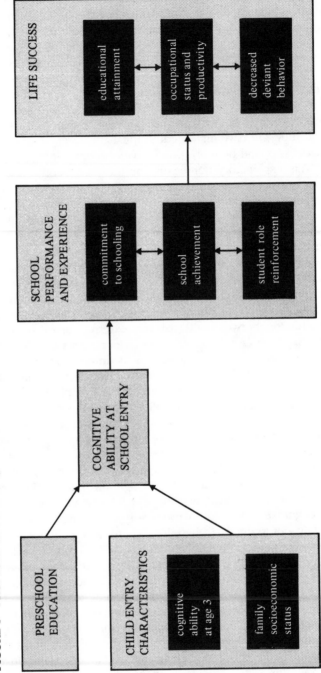

A second area of application is a transactional interpretation of the processes which constitute a child's school experience and performance. Here the issue shifts slightly, from heredity versus the environment to the individual versus the environment. Studies of the social aspects of the classroom have tended to focus almost exclusively on environmental influences on the child. A seminal though disputed work in this area was that of Rosenthal and Jacobson (1968) on teacher expectations as a determinant of student performance. In addition to technical problems with the research (Thorndike, 1968; Snow, 1969), the problem with their approach was that no attention was paid to the child's own attitudes and abilities. The excessiveness of their claims arose from their almost exclusive emphasis on teacher expectations.

Our transactional approach seeks to balance internal, self-originated motivations, attitudes, and abilities against external indications of expectation, approval, or disapproval. It places school achievement, the "data" to be interpreted, in the midst of these judgments by self and others. Judgments about how one is doing in school, made by self and by others, are based on feedback one obtains from the performance of school tasks. One's performance is *internally* generated, a product of abilities and motivations, and is evaluated by *external* standards; it is at the nexus between the individual and the school environment. This analysis then leads us to define three elements of school experience and performance: school achievement, commitment to schooling, and social reinforcement of the student role.

The transactional approach, as we have interpreted it here, distinguishing the internal and external processes of school experience, is very similar to a social-psychological "bonding" theory of the causes of delinquency advanced by Elliott, Ageton, and Canter (1979). While their purpose was to integrate various theories of delinquency causation, we believe that the resultant theoretical statements might well be viewed as transactional and may be helpful in interpreting the Perry Preschool study. They refer to the internal and external processes which form the bonds between the individual and the school. If these bonds are weak, the individual is a candidate for delinquent behavior. If these bonds are strong, the individual is more likely to avoid delinquent behavior and achieve greater adult success.

As the individual progresses through life, he or she passes through a series of environments, each of which stimulates and encourages abilities, motivations, and achievements in varying degrees. The individual comes to each environment anew, with some range of abilities and expectations. Then the individual interacts with the environment—demonstrating a way of performing, formulating a role and pattern of commitment, and quickly leading others into habitual patterns of response to him. The individual maintains this role from the inside; teachers, parents, and peers communicate expectations which maintain the individual in this role from the outside. While change in this role is possible, it is extremely difficult; better to begin with a role conducive to success. Preschool represents a period of time when such a role may be constructed through a high-quality educational program.

We will now explore the causal framework presented in figure 1.

Poverty

Poverty refers to a chronic condition characterized by a lack of money and material possessions and the related stress and constraints. While Lewis's (1959) notion of a culture of poverty is probably overstated, the persistence of the condition of poverty throughout lives and across generations is too often the case. Rainwater (1970) stresses the idea that the poor are marginal to the society, the disinherited outcasts who are blocked from entry into the mainstream.

Our concern is with the effects of poverty on children. Keniston (1977, p. 33) describes the world of poor children as "a world where even a small child learns to be ashamed of the way he or she lives. . . a world of intense social dangers, where many adults, driven by poverty and desperation, seem untrustworthy and unpredictable." Poor children are "systematically trained to fail" and many of them do fail in school, drop out of school, and wind up unemployed or marginally employed. Poor children run a high risk of failure in school (Jencks, Smith, Acland, Bane, Cohen, Gintis, Heyns, and Michelson, 1972; White, 1976, Note 4), particularly when they are black (Coleman, Campbell, Hobson, McPartland, Mood, Weinfeld, and York, 1966).

By focusing on the problems poor children experience, we do not mean to overlook the extent to which poor persons participate in the mainstream culture, nor the various strengths expressed by persons who happen to be poor, some of which are demanded for their very survival. Valentine and Valentine (1969, p. 412) reported the findings of one of their ethnographic studies of the poor:

> We see much energetic activity, great aesthetic and organizational variety, quite a number of highly patterned and well displayed behavior styles. Apathetic resignation does exist, but it is by no means the dominant tone of the community. Social disorganization can be found, but it occurs only within a highly structured context. Individual pathology is certainly present, but adaptive coping with adversity is more common. Positive strengths (often ignored in the literature) include the ability to deal with misfortune through humor, the capacity to respond to defeat with renewed effort, recourse to widely varied sacred and secular ideologies for psychological strengths, and resourceful devices to manipulate existing structures for maximum individual or group benefit. Perhaps least expectable from popular models is the capacity to mobilize initiatives for large-scale change like the movement for local control.

Despite these strengths, the poor have been unable for complex reasons to harness their energies to the conventional pathways to success—schooling and the workplace. This approach is passed on, to some extent, from parents to children.

Baratz and Baratz (1970) have argued that early childhood intervention is ethnocentric, in that it blames the victims of society for their impoverished condition and undermines their cultural values. Our opinion on this issue, in accord with our transactional approach, is that responsibility for the amelioration of poverty is shared by the poor person and by the society. Poor people are to some extent victims of society. But this victimization does not rob them completely of the capacity for action to improve their lot in life. Society has a collective responsibility to assist persons living in poverty in their own efforts to improve themselves. Early childhood intervention does not force children to improve; it gives children the opportunity for self-improvement. The distinction is a crucial one.

Children were selected for the Perry Preschool Project in part because they came from families that lived in poverty. Their socioeconomic standing was determined on the basis of their parents' low educational attainment (ninth grade average); unemployment (42 percent of the families had neither parent employed) or employment in unskilled labor (almost all of those who were employed); and high household density (a median of about seven persons in a five-room house). These facts make it clear that family incomes were low, were likely to remain low, and were inadequate to meet the needs of especially large families. Half the families received welfare assistance. About half were single-parent families, with only one adult to play the two roles of caregiver and breadwinner. In addition, they were black, in a country which discriminated against blacks.

Cognitive Ability

A transactional approach to cognitive ability emphasizes the notion that it is a balancing "between the action of the organism on the environment and vice versa" (Piaget, 1966, p. 7). It follows that children's cognitive abilities somehow reflect the environments in which they spend their time. Since children spend a good deal of time in school, the content and expectations of the school environment find their way into tests of cognitive ability, that is, IQ tests. Indeed, IQ tests were originally developed by Binet and Simon (1916) for the purpose of distinguishing retarded children from nonretarded children *in the school setting*. While cognitive ability may be in evidence in other settings, the IQ tests which are used to measure it most clearly focus on cognitive ability as it is realized in the school setting.

Children in the Perry Preschool study were selected in part because they performed with low cognitive ability on IQ tests given at age 3—in the borderline retarded range of 70 to 85. The average IQ of children of the lowest socioeconomic status is near the top of this range (Jensen, 1980, p. 44). Most members of the Perry sample, then, had IQs at age 3 that were below the average for their socioeconomic standing.

Cognitive Stimulation by Preschool Education

Webster's definition of *stimulate* is "to excite to activity or growth or to greater activity or exertion: stir up." By *cognitive stimulation* we mean the provision of opportunities for developmentally appropriate experiences which enhance cognitive performance. Stimulation need not be seen as a one-way effect of the environment on the organism, a concept that has been identified with behaviorist psychology. Building on Piaget's ideas, cognitive stimulation may be seen as a condition of more effective interaction between the child and the environment, interaction which is more effective because it leads the child to reaffirm his or her existing knowledge and to form new knowledge (that is, cognitive structures). Hunt (1961) was speaking of this sort of cognitive stimulation when he addressed the need to match up children with experience which challenged them to cognitive growth. Various curriculum models can provide cognitive stimulation in various ways (see Weikart, Epstein,

Schweinhart, & Bond, 1978). Currently, the curriculum approach of the High/Scope Foundation is to promote cognitive stimulation through a variety of key experiences for children (Hohmann, Banet, & Weikart, 1979).

There has been much discussion about whether there is some sensitive or critical period in the development of cognitive ability during early childhood (e.g., Bloom, 1964). There is a certain logical primacy of early experience in that causes must precede effects: almost the entire lives of children stretch before them. The most basic learning of one's life occurs during early childhood—essential cognitive structures and sensory organization are developed, as well as approaches to solving problems and the ability to generate language.

According to our interpretation of the data from the Perry Preschool study, the importance of this early intervention hinged as much on the fact that it preceded formal schooling as on some sensitive period of cognitive growth. The cognitive stimulation of an effective preschool program leads to an immediate increase in children's cognitive abilities. This enhanced cognitive ability is operational and highly visible at school entry, a time when the positions of children within the social system of the school are being determined, by themselves and others. Hence the children achieve more favorable positions and develop a greater commitment to schooling.

Cognitive Ability at School Entry

The importance of the impression a child creates at school entry was carefully documented in an ethnographic study of life in a kindergarten, with follow-up observations at first and second grade, by Rist (1971). Children in Rist's study were similar to the children in the Perry Preschool Project in that they were black and from families of lower socioeconomic status. Rist describes the process which he observed as follows: "There occurs within the classroom a social process whereby, out of a large group of children and an adult unknown to one another prior to the beginning of the school year, there emerge patterns of behavior, expectations of performance, and a mutually accepted stratification system delineating those who do well from those who do poorly" (pp. 71-72). The process was further delineated by Rist in five propositions, which might easily be adapted to what probably happened in the elementary-school aftermath of the Perry Preschool experience:

(1) The teacher constructs a model of success, largely related to social class.

(2) The teacher divides children into groups based on his or her evaluation of students at first meeting. In fact, Rist found that such groupings were made almost irrevocably *after only eight days of kindergarten.*

(3) The teacher treats groups very differently, liberally bestowing praise and high expectations on the group considered most likely to succeed, criticism and low expectations on the group considered most likely to fail. Classmates as well participate in these differential treatments.

(4) These interactional patterns become rigid and caste-like. This factor is the key to the long-term importance of the initial impression which the child makes.

(5) A similar process occurs in later years, only including the heritage of earlier years. Teachers communicate their expectations directly, to some extent. More importantly, children, their parents, and their peers maintain these expectations consistently and explicitly communicate them to teachers year after year.

It is reasonable to assume that the direct effects of preschool education are strongest immediately afterwards. The direct effect of preschool education of greatest consequence is increased cognitive ability. Our interpretative framework assigns to cognitive ability at school entry a special meaning in addition to its general meaning; greater cognitive ability seems to enhance children's entry into the social system of the school, putting them in a better position than they would otherwise be in, a position which is highly stable and persistent.

The School Success Flow

Early in his or her school career, the child takes on a relatively permanent role or position in terms of success or failure. This process is characterized by some degree of participation in the *school success flow*. School is the basic success-defining institution in the lives of children, virtually the only institution outside the family in which they have extensive experience (see Gold, 1978). The "success flow" notion assumes that a level of school success or failure remains constant over long periods of time. We attribute such stability to the routinized patterns of social dynamics postulated in role theories applied to the classroom (e.g., Jackson, 1968). However, we would complement their focus on external dynamics with an additional focus on personal, internal dynamics, involving abilities and motivations (Elliott, Ageton, & Canter, 1979). We have identified three elements of the process: commitment to schooling, school achievement, and social reinforcement of the student role.

Commitment to Schooling

Personal commitment to schooling is a concept meant to encompass the set of attitudes and motivations which define the child's relationship to the school. The child's commitment to the institution may be seen as the basic motivation for ongoing school-related behavior. Commitment to one's personal future in the school success flow may be viewed as aspiration, or ambition, whose importance as a determinant of future position has been attested to by Turner (1964) and Rehberg and Rosenthal (1978). In the theory proposed by Elliott et al. (1979), personal commitment is the internal aspect of the process of bonding between the individual and the school.

In the Perry Preschool study, the child's personal commitment to schooling was measured in elementary school by teacher ratings of the child's school motivation and at age 15 by the youths' own assessments of the value they placed on schooling, their thoughts about college, and the amount of homework they did.

School Achievement

School achievement reflects the extent to which students meet the commonly accepted objectives of schooling. The most widely accepted objectives of schooling are that students learn to read, write, and speak properly, and to carry out arithmetic operations with accuracy. These are the skills that standardized tests of school achievement claim to assess, and these are the skills that teachers are most likely to regard as evidence of school success.

The person who is highly committed to schooling and who receives social reinforcement for a success-oriented student role is, of course, the one most likely to meet the objectives of schooling and do well in terms of school achievement. But it is equally true that the person who does well in terms of school achievement, all other things being equal, is most likely to become more committed to schooling and to receive social reinforcement for a success-oriented student role. Motivation, performance, and social support are simply analytic, conceptual distinctions which cannot be separated in practice; that is, it could not be said that one of them causes another in a one-way flow from cause to effect. They all constitute an experiential, dynamic transaction between the individual and the environment.

School achievement was assessed in the Perry Preschool study by standardized tests of school achievement given annually from the end of first grade through the end of fifth grade and again at the end of eighth grade.

Social Reinforcement of the Student Role

Jackson (1968) identifies a number of characteristics that constitute performance of a student role in a classroom: ability to ignore distractions and interruptions, ability to be patient and cope with delay, recognition of the much greater power and authority of the teacher compared to oneself, and adaptation to a pervasive *spirit of evaluation* that dominates one's school career. We are particularly concerned with this spirit of evaluation, the orientation of the student towards school success or failure. In the words of Gold (1978, p. 25): "Achievement is the core of the student role in American society, and in no other role are the standards of achievement so clear or the means to attain them so narrow. Experiences of success and failure pervade student life."

The incipient ways of treating students documented by Rist (1971) are the beginnings of the social reinforcement of the student role. Students perform differently and are treated differently throughout schooling. In addition, grouping and tracking procedures, within and beyond the classroom, constitute a powerful means of defining roles along a full range from school success to school failure (see, for example, Schafer & Olexa, 1971). Parents and peers tend to follow the lead of the teachers in this regard, since teachers are widely recognized as the arbiters of school success and failure.

One of the most powerful means of social reinforcement of school success or failure at the teacher's disposal is assignment to a regular classroom, retention in grade, or assignment to some sort of special education. The primary reason for grade retention or special education assignment is that they are for the good of the child and the class. It is nearly pointless to place a child in a regular classroom where he or she is gaining nothing from the instructional process and may in fact be disrupting this process for other students. A child in need of special services has a right to them, in principle and in actual legislation. But grade retention and, to a greater extent, receipt of special education services unmistakably label a child as a scholastic failure. This message is not a one-time occurrence; it is communicated day in and day out, over months and years, in ordinary conversation, in the instructional process and the communication of expectations, and in the very structure of the school building. Though one may get extra attention from a specially trained teacher, the psychic price is very great.

In the Perry Preschool study, the number of years during which a child received special education was used as an index of the type of social reinforcements a student received from teachers. Reinforcements from parents were assessed by the parent's stated satisfaction with the child's school performance and by the parent's scholastic aspirations for the child. Reinforcements by peers were measured by the rated social status of the child during elementary school.

Life Success

We are using the term life success in a very broad sense to refer to demonstrable accomplishments (or failures) beyond school experience and performance which have implications for the quality of one's life. The most frequently used index of life success is some variant of the occupational status or income of individuals or families (for example, Jencks et al., 1979). We are including educational attainment (years of schooling) in this domain as a major bridge between the school success flow and subsequent life success. We are also including deviant behavior—school disciplinary problems, delinquent and criminal activities. Deviant behavior constitutes evidence of a kind of failure, clearly recognized as such by society, if not always by the individual.

School Failure and Deviant Behavior

Hirschi (1969) defined delinquent acts as behavior whose detection ". . . is thought to result in punishment of the person committing them by agents of the larger society" (p. 47). This definition is readily expanded to other deviant acts of concern to us. School disciplinary problems are simply acts fitting the above definition in the school context. Criminal acts differ from delinquent acts in that the offender is considered an adult rather than a juvenile; hence criminal acts are not considered here.

However, our concern should perhaps be directed not so much to the one-time offender whose offense is something of a "lark." From the viewpoint of longitudinal research, a more important concern is a sustained pattern of delinquency—repeated or even chronic deviant acts. As Becker (1963) puts it: "We are not so much interested in the person who commits a deviant act once as in a person who sustains a pattern of deviance over a long period of time, who makes of deviance a way of life, who organizes his identity around a pattern of deviant behavior" (p. 30). This line of thinking suggests a fruitful approach to analysis of cases across variables, which will be pursued in future research. The principal implication for the present report is that the pattern of *repeated* delinquent offenses is the condition to be studied.

There exists a wealth of data which demonstrates a strong relationship between school failure and delinquency (Conger & Miller, 1966; Elliott & Voss, 1974; Hargreaves, 1967; Hirschi, 1969; Polk & Schafer, 1972; Rhodes & Reiss, 1969; Wolfgang, Figlio, & Sellin, 1972). As Gold has said (1978, pp. 292-293): ". . . a major provocation for delinquent behavior is incompetence in the role of student and its adjunct roles in the school."

The elements in our analysis of the school success flow—commitment to schooling, school achievement, and social reinforcement of the student role—are closely related to the bonding explanation of delinquency (Hirschi, 1969; Elliott, Ageton, & Canter, 1979). Elliott et al. (1979) identify commitment as the internal aspect of social bonding and the adoption of a role as the external aspect of social bonding. When these bonds are strong, delinquency is unlikely. When they are weak, delinquency may well result. While neither Elliott nor Hirschi include cognitive ability or school achievement in their formulation of the bonding explanation of delinquency, Hirschi and Hindelang (1977) have indicated that cognitive ability does have a role in the etiology of delinquency. Silverberg and Silverberg (1971) make a similar case for school achievement.

In the Perry Preschool study through age 15, school conduct and delinquent behavior in the community were assessed through the self-reports of members of the sample. Elliott and Voss (1974, pp. 64-92) present convincing arguments that self-report data have a number of advantages over official records of delinquency, basically because they represent delinquent acts themselves rather than the process of being apprehended for committing delinquent acts.

School Success and Occupational Status

In sociological terms, the American dream is that upward economic mobility in this country may be realized through educational attainment and hard work. In the past decade or so, the reality of this promise has been challenged by a revisionist group of historians (Katz, 1968; Karier, 1975; Feinberg, 1975) and social scientists (e.g., Bowles & Gintis, 1976). More recently, the Carnegie Council on Children has become party to this critique (Keniston, 1977; Ogbu, 1978; deLone, 1978). The principal focus of the Carnegie Council has been to define the seriousness of the needs of children and the relationship of these needs to the broader domestic issues of the society. Their call to improve the quality of life for children by means of structural, family-oriented changes in adult society is an important position on a previously neglected side of the issues. Their cautions about the limited effectiveness of social and educational programs in effecting change are a way to make more realistic the naive optimism of the 1960s in this regard. But it is important to distinguish between caution and despair.

DeLone's critique of schooling can be taken as representative of the others. DeLone challenged the belief "that the skills schools teach (or children learn) play a direct and critical role in preparing children for adult success, especially occupational success" (p. 98). He argued that the relationships found between school achievement tests and career success are weak. He dismissed educational attainment as the *credentialing effect;* that is, he attributed the importance of educational attainment to the fact that schools confer diplomas, not that they impart useful skills or knowledge (see also Collins, 1979).

Ravitch, in her book *The Revisionists Revised* (1977), has countered this position with a most articulate defense of the promise of upward economic mobility through educational attainment. First, there is the fact of persistent upward economic mobility in our society. Second, there is a strong contribution of educational attainment to upward economic mobility. Jencks et al. (1972), despite interpretations of their work to the contrary, made this point on the basis of a review of empirical studies: "Educational attainment is one of the prime determinants of occupational status" (p. 185); and Jencks et al. (1979) reaffirmed the point on the basis of an even more thorough and systematic review.

Finally, with regard to the so-called credentialling effect, it seems to us that the conferring of diplomas is simply the culmination of an evaluative process that permeates the process of schooling. The transactional model suggests strongly that such evaluation constitutes an appraisal of the student's school performance and role, rather than some capricious sorting. Likewise, educational attainment is a reflection of a student's role, achievement, and commitment to schooling. Since the school is the principal if not the only institution defining success and failure for children, staying in school long enough to be credentialled may be the best evidence a student can provide to an employer that he or she accepts mainstream values and is likely to succeed in a job.

Since this report follows young people only to age 15, educational attainment and adult occupational status have not been measured or reported here. Both will be reported in a subsequent monograph, which will follow youths through age 19. The only source of evidence in this matter reported here is their employment status when they were 15 years old.

The Framework in Perspective

This chapter has presented a conception of a chain of causes and effects beginning with early childhood experience and ending with "life success." This conceptual framework is meant to set the stage for the presentation of the design and results of the Perry Preschool Project through age 15. We have postponed a discussion of other early childhood intervention research to the last chapter.

Our basic approach has been transactional, emphasizing the changing relationship between the individual and the environment over time. The analysis began with children in poverty. Despite a variety of adaptive strengths, the poor child experiences conditions which inhibit development and may lead to school failure. Preschool education provides extra cognitive stimulation for such children, leading them to demonstrate greater cognitive ability at school entry. Then the rigid stratification process of the school takes over, and they must assume defined positions with respect to school success or failure. Throughout their years of schooling, they perform in terms of this student role—believing it themselves, forming a level of commitment to schooling consistent with their expectations for success or failure, and even attaining a level of school achievement consistent with their expected position. Teachers, parents, and peers accept this position and reinforce it, so that everyone, including the child, has similar expectations and supporting attitudes for the child's scholastic accomplishments. Eventually, school success becomes life success. To the extent that the child has been successful in school, the adult is successful in educational attainment, occupational status, and income. To the extent that the child has failed in school, the adolescent, aided and abetted by like-minded peers, finds it reasonable to assault the school and the community through deviant behavior—demanding, in the final analysis, a degree of attention denied by all the conventional channels for approval.

II. Design of the Perry Preschool Project

The Perry Preschool Project is an examination of the lives of children who were born with the odds against them—poor, apparently destined for school failure, and black in a country which discriminated against blacks. These children were assigned to either an experimental group or a control group so that groups were similar on a variety of background characteristics. The experimental group received a preschool education program of one or two years' duration. The control group received no preschool program. These two groups of children have now been studied continuously for almost two decades.

The study was conducted with children born in Ypsilanti, Michigan. The population of the city and township of Ypsilanti, according to the 1970 Census, was 62,732, of whom 13 percent were black. Here and throughout southeastern Michigan, the principal industry is the manufacture of automobiles, with over 25,000 employees in the Ypsilanti area. The other major activity in the area is higher education, with 25,000 students in Ypsilanti at Eastern Michigan University and Washtenaw Community College and an additional 35,000 ten miles away in Ann Arbor (1970 population 99,797) at the University of Michigan. While the children in the study lived in poverty, they were surrounded by relative affluence. Among 332 counties in the nation with over 50,000 people in the 1970 Census, their home county of Washtenaw ranked thirty-first in median family income.

The longitudinal sample was drawn from children who lived in the attendance area of the Perry Elementary School, on the south side of Ypsilanti. A 1952 report of the Ypsilanti Housing Commission called it "one of the worst congested slum areas in the State of Michigan." School failure and a high crime rate have been perennial problems in the area.

Children with the Odds Against Them

The poorest children in the neighborhood were selected for the longitudinal sample, 123 children who entered life with all the odds against their success. Children were selected from five age cohorts born each year between 1958 and 1962 whose names appeared on the family census of the Perry Elementary School or who were referred by neighborhood groups or who were found by a door-to-door search. The first criterion for selection was that parents reported a low socioeconomic status.* The second criterion for selection was that children's IQs, tested at project entry by the Stanford-Binet Scale, were in the range of 70 to 85.

The poverty and lack of schooling of families in the sample are illustrated in table 1, by comparisons with blacks and the total population nationally. These parents had an overall median of 9.4 years of school, slightly less than the national figure for blacks, but over two and a half years below the overall national figure. Less than one in five of the parents had completed high school, compared to one in two nationally. About half the families in the sample were single-head families, compared to one in seven nationally; not surprisingly, single-head families accounted for most of the unemployment among families in the sample.

---

*Socioeconomic status was computed as the sum of scores, standardized within the sample, for: (1) the average of parents' years of school, (2) the father's (or single mother's) employment level, and (3) half of the ratio of rooms per person in the household (see Weikart, Bond, & McNeil, 1978 for details).

18

TABLE 1 FAMILY DEMOGRAPHIC COMPARISONS: LONGITUDINAL SAMPLE AND UNITED STATES

Category	Sample at Project Entry 1962-65	United States (1970 Census) Blacks	All Races
Schooling of Parents			
Mothers/Females 25 and over:			
Median years of school	9.7	10.0	12.1
Elementary	32%	41%	27%
Some high school	47%	26%	20%
High school completed	21%	33%	53%
Fathers/Males 25 and over:			
Median years of school	8.8	9.6	11.8
Elementary	46%	45%	27%
Some high school	43%	23%	19%
High school completed	11%	32%	54%
Family Composition & Employment			
Husband-wife families	53%[a,b]	69%	86%
Both employed	7%	29%	29%
One only employed	38%	30%	46%
None employed[c]	7%	9%	11%
Single-head families[d]	47%[b]	33%	14%
Head employed	13%	17%	8%
None employed	34%	16%	6%
All families			
Employed adult male	50%	60%	74%
Employed adult female	20%[e]	47%	38%
None employed[c]	42%	25%	17%
Receiving welfare assistance	50%	18%	5%
Employment level for working adult males: Professional	0%[f]	9%	25%
Skilled	5%	25%	39%
Semiskilled	14%	30%	20%
Unskilled	81%	35%	16%
Household Density			
Median persons	6.7	3.1	2.7
Median rooms	4.8	4.7	4.8
Person/room ratio	1.24	.66	.56
Ratio greater than 1.00	63%	19%	8%

[a]The 123 children in the sample comprised 100 families due to siblings, but 123 cases were used in calculations because child conditions were being reported. The experimental group had 6 sibling pairs, one group of 3, and one group of 4. The control group had 12 sibling pairs.

[b]In 1973-77, when youths were 15, the sample had 42 percent husband-wife families and 58 percent single-head families.

[c]Labor force participation of unemployed persons was ignored in these categorizations.

[d]Nationally 11 percent of families have a single female head and 3 percent a single male head.

[e]In 1973-77, when youths were 15, the sample had 45 percent of mothers employed.

[f]Based on 66 working fathers in the sample. The employmment level of mothers in the sample was either unskilled or not reported.

In two out of five families in the sample, no one was employed. When parents in the sample were employed, their employment level was usually unskilled. Half of the families in the sample received welfare assistance, compared to only one in twenty families nationally. They lived in residences that were typical in size but crowded, with over twice the number of people in the typical household.

When tested at project entry, the children in the sample were found to have IQs in the range of 70 to 85, with a mean of 79. In accord with the guidelines of the American Association for Mental Deficiency prevailing at that time (Heber, 1961) as well as the State of Michigan guidelines, they were classified as borderline "educable mentally retarded" by state-certified school psychologists. Since that time, official definitions have changed so that IQs in this range are no longer regarded as evidence of handicap (Grossman, 1973). This change reflects in part an ongoing controversy about the meaning of the IQ test for black children.

Prior to the 1960s, the IQ test was often assumed to be an unbiased measure of intelligence, a trait which many assumed to be genetically determined. The total genetic determination of intelligence was challenged by various educational intervention studies of the 1960s. But when IQ gains disappeared, Jensen (1969) renewed the previous claims about intelligence and unleashed a storm of controversy that is still raging. A principal issue has been how to interpret the fact that blacks on the average score 12 points lower than whites on IQ tests (Jensen, 1980, pp. 43 and 99). On this basis, one would expect almost half of all blacks to be at or below the IQ of 85, which was formerly the upper limit defining educable mental retardation.

It is generally accepted that the cognitive ability measured by IQ tests comes in part from one's genetic makeup, in part from one's prior experience, and in part from the cognitive stimulation in one's present environment. We maintain, in disagreement with Jensen, that a 12 point IQ difference may be attributed solely to the nature of one's present environment. A lifetime of inferior schooling, scholastic and occupational failure, crowded housing conditions, and overt discrimination could easily lead to depressed cognitive ability. If a preschool program provided increased opportunity for effective interaction between an individual and the environment, a concurrent increase in cognitive ability would result. Likewise, if an elementary school or high school provided greater opportunity for such interaction (appropriate to the child's stage of development), then it might also lead to concurrent gains in cognitive ability.

All members of the sample were black, during a period which may come to be seen as a historical watershed for blacks. Living conditions for their parents were not much better than they had been for their grandparents or great-grandparents. They had never really recovered from their heritage of enslavement and the stereotypes used to justify it. Then came the civil rights movement, with its demands for black equality and eventually the laws to back up these demands.

The children of the Perry Preschool study, after the early intervention program, went to schools that were partially subsidized by federal and state compensatory education funds. They witnessed national movements towards school desegregation, open housing, and equal employment opportunity. By 1980 some real progress has been made, not only in the enactment of laws, but also in the schooling, housing, employment, and income acquired by some blacks. On the whole, blacks are still far from equality in these categories. But the absolute barriers of overt discrimination have been removed. As the children of the Perry study become adults, role models for black success are increasing, and the pathways to success are becoming more visible for them.

The Design: Experimental Versus Control Group

Children entered the project in five waves, as outlined in table 2. Each wave of children was a year younger than the preceding wave, with the oldest born in 1958 and the youngest born in 1962. The project began in 1962 with the selection of a group of four-year-olds designated Wave Zero and a group of three-year-olds designated Wave One. The sample was completed over the next three years by the annual selection of three more waves of three-year-old children— Waves Two, Three and Four. This wave design allowed the study to employ approximate replications of the basic treatment, thereby increasing confidence that results will generalize to other replications of the basic treatment, rather than being limited to precise duplication.

Each year, children in the sample for that year were assigned either to the experimental group or to the control group in such a way as to equate groups on the basis of initial cognitive ability, sex ratios, and average socioeconomic status of the groups. First, the children were ranked by their initial IQs; even rankings were assigned to one group and odd rankings to the other. Pairs of similarly ranked children were exchanged between groups until the sex ratios and mean socioeconomic-status scores for the two groups were equivalent. Then one of these groups was arbitrarily designated the experimental group and the other the control group. In Waves Two, Three, and Four, any child with an older sibling in the experimental group was assigned to the experimental group, and any child with an older sibling in the control group was assigned to the control group. This procedure was meant to ensure that the preschool education received by a child (with the mother's participation) in the experimental group

TABLE 2 PARTICIPANT AGE BY CALENDAR YEAR

Year	Wave Zero	One	Two	Three	Four	
1958	0					
1959	1	0				
1960	2	1	0			
1961	3	2	1	0		
1962	4	3	2	1	0	
1963	5	4	3	2	1	
1964	6	5	4	3	2	
1965	7	6	5	4	3	
1966	8	7	6	5	4	Preschool Years
1967	9	8	7	6	5	
1968	10	9	8	7	6	Elementary School Years
1969	11	10	9	8	7	
1970	12	11	10	9	8	
1971	13	12	11	10	9	
1972	14	13	12	11	10	
1973	15	14	13	12	11	
1974	16	15	14	13	12	
1975	17	16	15	14	13	Middle School Years
1976	18	17	16	15	14	
1977	19	18	17	16	15	
1978	20	19	18	17	16	High School Years
1979	21	20	19	18	17	
1980	22	21	20	19	18	

would not have an indirect effect on a sibling in the control group (see table 1, note *a*). Finally, in a slight deviation from random assignment techniques, five children were transferred from the experimental group to the control group, rather than dropped from the study, because they were unable to attend preschool or to participate with their mothers in the home-visit component of the program. These children came from single-parent families in which the mother was employed. These procedures resulted in the sample sizes of groups within the waves documented in table 3.

TABLE 3   NUMBER OF CASES IN LONGITUDINAL SAMPLE: GROUP BY WAVE

Wave	Sample	Experimental Group	Control Group
Total Sample	123	58	65
Wave Zero	28	13	15
Wave One	17	8	9
Wave Two	26	12	14
Wave Three	27	13	14
Wave Four	25	12	13

Equivalence of the Experimental and Control Groups

The pattern of outcome differences found in the study is definitely due to preschool education. This high degree of certainty is based on three facts: (a) a close approximation to random assignment of children in the experimental and control groups, (b) the equivalence of the two groups on almost all background characteristics, as described below, and (c) the consistency of findings favoring preschool education, as reported previously and in the next chapters. This study came closer than most field studies in education to achieving the goal of true experimental design. In terms employed by Campbell and Stanley (1963), it has strong internal validity, meaning that the inferences drawn from the study very probably do mean what they seem to mean.*

The experimental group and the control group were equivalent on a variety of background characteristics, that is, variables which served to locate children and families within the socioeconomic matrix and which could not reasonably be expected to be affected by preschool education. Apparently the cautious matching procedure employed in this study was sufficient to ensure the equivalence of the two groups.

---

*A brief note should be injected at this point concerning the reporting of group differences in the tables and figures of this report, matters explained more fully in the appendix. For each test of statistical significance, the exact p value is reported if it was less than .100, that is, less than 1 in 10. The p value is the probability, expressed as a proportion of 1.000, that (in this case) the group difference on the variable occurred by chance. When the p value is reported, it is accompanied by the percent of variance accounted for by group membership. The percent of variance estimates the magnitude or strength of association between two variables, in this case, between receiving or not receiving preschool education and the outcome variable. If some set of variables accounted for 100 percent of the variance in some outcome variable, then an individual's scores on that set of variables would perfectly predict that individual's score on the outcome variable.

As shown in table 4, groups were equivalent on all measures of youth background and on almost all measures of family background. The two groups of youths were equivalent in sex ratio, age at project entry, family size, birth order, and IQ at project entry. Families in the two groups were equivalent at project entry in socioeconomic status, median years of school completed by mothers and by fathers, proportion of two-parent versus single-parent families, employment status in two-parent families, welfare status, employment levels of employed fathers, and household density.

When interviewed eleven years later, families in the two groups were equivalent on all of the demographic characteristics measured: proportion of two-parent versus single-parent families, employment status of mothers and fathers in both types of families, household density, neighborhood rating by parents, and number of family moves since the child started school. The only group difference in any demographic characteristic was that, at project entry only, more control-group mothers in single-parent families were employed, a difference unquestionably due to the practice of reassigning children with single mothers employed outside the home to the control group. However, the difference in mothers' employment status was temporary, probably only while children were young, since there was no difference 11 years after project entry. The experimental and control groups became, if anything, more alike in demographic characteristics over time.

Preschool Education and Home Visits

Children in the experimental group attended a group preschool program 12½ hours a week (weekday mornings) and were visited along with their mothers at home 1½ hours a week. This routine was maintained for about 30 weeks a year, from mid-October through the end of May. The experimental group in Wave Zero received the program for one school year, the remaining waves for two school years.

Each year there were 4 teachers responsible for 20 to 25 children in the classroom, a teacher-child ratio of 1 to 5 or 6.* The 10 persons who served as teachers during the project were all female; 3 were black. One teacher remained through the 5 years of the project; 3 remained 2 to 3 years; and 6 stayed 1 to 2 years. In addition to the project director (Weikart), an additional 2 or 3 researchers were generally assigned to the project, with 9 persons occupying these positions between 1962 and 1967.

The goal of the Perry Preschool's educational program was to help children acquire the intellectual strengths they would need in school. Throughout the operation of the program, teachers and staff were enthusiastic about this goal and employed a variety of strategies in their attempts to meet it. In the first years, strategies were as likely as not to use paper and pencil and to focus on the alphabet, colors, and shapes. But the traditional nursery school emphasis on direct manipulation of materials also had its proponents. In the second year of the project, the staff learned of the Swiss psychologist Jean Piaget and his explanation of how children's development is related to their experience. Piaget saw language and rational thought as closely related to sensory and motor

---

*By comparison, the National Day Care Study recommended a maximum of 18 preschoolers per classroom and a staff-child ratio of 1 to 7 (Ruopp, Travers, Glantz, & Coelen, 1979).

**TABLE 4   DEMOGRAPHIC COMPARISONS:
EXPERIMENTAL VS. CONTROL GROUP**

Category	Experimental Group	Control Group	p[a]	Var
Number of cases (youths)[b]	58	65		
Gender: Percent female	43%	40%	—	
Age at entry—Wave 0	4.4	4.2	—	
Waves 1-4	3.3	3.3	—	
Number of children in family[c]	5.7	5.8	—	
Siblings older than youth	2.8	3.0	—	
Stanford-Binet IQ at entry	79.8	78.5	—	
Median years of school of parents				
Mothers	10.0	9.5	—	
Fathers	8.6	9.0	—	
Families[d]				
Socioeconomic status[e]	8.00	7.92	—	
Receiving welfare assistance	55%	45%	—	
No parent employed	51%	34%		
Two-parent families	*54%*	*51%*	—	
Mother works	5%	9%	—	
Father works	46%	45%	—	
Employment level— Skilled	4%	2%	—	
Semiskilled	10%	3%	—	
Unskilled	32%	40%		
Female-headed families	*46%*	*49%*	—	
Mother works	4%	22%	.002	12.7%
Families 11 years later[c]				
No parent employed[f]	46%	40%	—	
Two-parent families	*39%*	*42%*	—	
Mother works	10%	6%	—	
Father works	32%	38%	—	
Female-headed families	*61%*	*58%*	—	
Mother works	17%	20%	—	
Housing				
Person/room ratio	1.20	1.25	—	
Neighborhood rating by parent:[c]				
Excellent	21%	15%	—	
Good	45%	46%		
Fair	13%	19%		
Not so good	13%	7%		
Poor	9%	13%		
Family moves since child started school[c] 0	15%	17%	—	
1	58%	54%		
2-4	27%	30%		

[a]The two-tailed p value, based on the chi-square test, was reported if less than .10, followed by the percent of variance accounted for by group membership.

[b]Data collected at project entry, 1962-65, unless otherwise noted.

[c]Data collected 11 years after program entry, 1973-1977.

[d]The 123 youths in the sample comprised 100 families due to siblings; 123 cases were used in these calculations because child conditions are being reported.

[e]SES = scores standardized within the sample for: average of parents' years in school, average of parents' levels of employment, and half of rooms per person in households.

[f]Labor force participation of unemployed persons was ignored in these calculations.

experience. Also, a consulting visit from Israeli psychologist Sara Smilansky helped to crystallize the notion that the child would plan some of his or her own activities every day. The teachers' role was to help the child think through and articulate these plans and activities.

A key to the growth of this curriculum model, now known as the High/Scope Cognitively Oriented Curriculum, was the continued interaction of teachers and researchers. Teachers learned that they had to justify their practices and that they had to work within a group rather than as isolated individuals. Researchers likewise learned the importance of justifying their ideas, translating them into practical terms, and respecting the experience of teachers as a primary source of knowledge about education. The curriculum model that emerged from the Perry Preschool Project was documented by Weikart, Rogers, Adcock, and McClelland (1970). However, even before that book was published, the curriculum model continued to evolve towards inclusion of the child in the planning of program activities and towards a focus on learning directly from concrete experience and its expression in language. The Cognitively Oriented Curriculum as it is now conceived and practiced is to be found in the book *Young Children in Action* by Hohmann, Banet, and Weikart (1979).

The Data: 48 Measures with Low Attrition

This report is based on data collected from or about members of the sample between ages 3 and 15, with its major focus on data from youth and parent interviews collected when youths were 15 and from an IQ test and a school achievement test administered when youths were 14. The sources of data for this report are listed in table 5. Parents completed an initial interview and another interview 11 years later. Youths received IQ tests annually from ages 3 to 10 and at age 14; they received school achievement tests annually from ages 7 to 11 and at age 14. Two child rating scales were filled out by teachers at kindergarten, first, second, and third grades. School records from kindergarten through high school were examined. At age 15 youths were interviewed extensively. (A comprehensive assessment at age 19 is currently underway and is scheduled for completion in 1981.)

The original sample at project entry of 128 children was reduced to a longitudinal sample of 123. In the experimental group, 3 children moved out of the area before they completed the program. In the control group, 1 child died, and 1 child moved out of the area shortly after project entry and was not followed up.

In almost two decades since the end of preschool, there has been almost no absolute attrition of subjects from the sample; that is, they can all still be located and assessed. This lack of attrition is reflected in a very low rate of missing data across the 48 measures in the study through age 15. The median rate of missing data across these measures is only 5 percent. For only 4 measures do missing data exceed 25 percent. Also, the relative homogeneity of the sample militates against differential attrition across groups. Such low rates of missing data have virtually no harmful effect on statistical analysis.

The lack of sample attrition reflects a strong tendency for Ypsilanti residents to remain in Ypsilanti and the surrounding area. One reason for this stability is the presence of the automobile industry, creating a specialized and geographically contained job market. The lack of sample attrition also reflects

TABLE 5   SOURCES OF DATA FOR THIS REPORT[a]

Topic	Table (T) or Figure (F)	Measure	Age of Youth
demographics	T 1, 4	PI-1	3
		PI-2	15
		1970 U.S. Census	
group size and chronology	T 2, 3	project records	
attrition	T 6		
IQ	F 2	Binet	3-10[b]
		WISC	14
school achievement	F 3, 4, 5	CAT	7-11, 14
school commitment	T 7, 8	YRS, PBI	6-9
		YI	15
special education	F 6	school records	6-18
social status	—	YRS, PBI	6-9
parent on youth's schooling	T 9	YRS, YI, PI-2	6-9, 15
school conduct	T 10	PBI, YI	6-9, 15
delinquent behavior	F 7, T 11	YI	15
youth employment	T 12	YI	15
self concept	T 13	YI	15
parent-youth relationship	T 14	YI, PI-2	15
youth social patterns	—	YI	15
youth use of time	—	YI	15
parent use of time	—	PI-2	15
causal analysis	F 8	all sources	

LEGEND

PI-1: Initial Parent Interview
PI-2: Second Parent Interview
Binet: Stanford-Binet Intelligence Scale (Terman & Merrill, 1960)
WISC: Wechsler Intelligence Scale for Children (Wechsler, 1949)
CAT: California Achievement Tests (Tiegs & Clark, 1963, 1970)
YRS: Ypsilanti Rating Scale
PBI: Pupil Behavior Inventory (Vinter, Sarri, Vorwaller, & Shafer, 1966)
YI: Youth Interview (based in part on Bachman, O'Malley, & Johnston, 1978)

[a] Data collected but not reported here included: hospital records, the Maternal Attitude Inventory (from Schaefer & Bell, 1958), the Cognitive Home Environment Scale (from Wolf, 1964, Note 5), the Adapted Leiter International Performance Scale (Arthur, 1952), the Illinois Test of Psycholinguistic Abilities (experimental version; McCarthy & Kirk, 1961), and the Peabody Picture Vocabulary Test (Dunn, 1965). Findings for these data were reported by Weikart, Bond, and McNeil (1978).
[b] A dash indicates *annual* assessments between the indicated ages.

our continuous contact with members of the sample—almost every year. It reflects extraordinary efforts by interviewers and testers skilled in investigative tracking. Most importantly, it reflects the continued cooperation and good will of the community, schools, parents, and the subjects themselves.

For the four instruments featured in this report, the proportions of missing cases were somewhat higher than was typical throughout the study: 11 percent on the WISC IQ test and 23 percent on the California Achievement Test given at age 14; and 20 percent on the youth interview and 17 percent on the parent interview given when youths were 15 years old. Table 6 presents an analysis of potential differential attrition across groups for these instruments. The first

**TABLE 6   ANALYSIS OF DIFFERENTIAL ATTRITION
FOR AGE 14-15 INSTRUMENTS**

Instrument	Background Variables					
Group/Status on Instrument	N/% of Group[a]	Females	Initial IQ	Socio-economic Status	Single-parent	Mother's Schooling
Age 14 IQ	**110/89%**					
Experimental/Present	54/93%	44%	79.5	8.02	47%	9.4
Control/Present	56/86%	39%	78.0	7.82	50%	9.3
Experimental/Absent	4/ 7%	25%	80.0	7.75	25%	10.5
Control/Absent	9/14%	44%	81.9	8.56	45%	10.1
p	—	—	—	—	—	—
Age 14 Achievement	**95/77%**					
Experimental/Present	49/84%	45%	80.0	8.06	48%	9.8
Control/Present	46/71%	39%	78.4	7.80	48%	9.3
Experimental/Absent	9/16%	33%	77.0	7.67	33%	7.7
Control/Absent	19/29%	42%	78.8	8.21	53%	9.7
p	.070	—	—	—	—	.051
Youth Interview	**99/80%**					
Experimental/Present	44/76%	41%	79.1	8.07	49%	9.7
Control/Present	55/85%	40%	78.4	7.84	51%	9.2
Experimental/Absent	14/24%	50%	81.1	7.79	36%	8.6
Control/Absent	10/15%	40%	79.3	8.40	40%	10.2
p	—	—	—	—	—	—
Parent Interview	**102/83%**					
Experimental/Present	48/83%	42/5	79.2	8.10	49%	9.6
Control/Present	54/83%	39%	78.7	7.85	50%	9.3
Experimental/Absent	10/17%	50%	81.4	7.50	30%	8.6
Control/Absent	11/17%	45%	77.9	8.27	45%	10.0
p	—	—	—	—	—	—

[a] Chi-square analysis of numbers in groups compares the experimental and the control group. Other tests, based on analysis of variance, compare all four groups listed; p is listed when it is less than .100.

question was whether the experimental and control groups differed in the proportion of cases for whom data on the instrument were present or absent. There were no differences for the IQ test or either of the interviews. However, a larger proportion of the experimental group took the achievement test at age 14 (84 percent vs. 71 percent).

When compared on a number of background variables—sex ratio, initial cognitive ability, socioeconomic status, proportion of single-parent families, and mothers' years of school—groups were equivalent on all variables for the IQ test and youth and parent interviews; groups were equivalent on all variables except mother's schooling for the school achievement test. Further analysis of mother's schooling for the school achievement test revealed that, while experimental-group mothers with the least schooling were not represented among those who took the test, the experimental- and control-group members who took the test did not differ in their mother's years of schooling.* It seems reasonable to

---

*A statement that groups did not differ on a variable is made in this report only when the probability of chance occurrence of the difference found was greater than 1 in 10 (that is, $p > .100$).

conclude that differential attrition was not likely to have distorted comparisons of outcomes for the experimental group and the control group for the instruments used at ages 14 and 15.

The same six interviewers were assigned equally to the experimental group and the control group for the youth interviews and the parent interviews. These interviewers each conducted between 11 and 24 percent of the parent interviews and between 16 and 39 percent of the youth interviews (except for two of them who interviewed one and two youths respectively). There were no group differences in who the respondent was for the parent interviews: for the sample as a whole, 88 percent of the respondents to the parent interview were mothers, 8 percent were other female guardians, and 4 percent were fathers.

Further validation of the age 15 youth interview came from interviewer judgments of the youths during the interviews. The interviewer completed 9 such items after each interview. Items reflected the interviewee's responsiveness, appearance, ability to communicate, and apparent acceptance of middle-class values.* There were no group differences for the scale as a whole or for any item on the scale.

Since interviewers had no knowledge of the group membership of subjects, their objectivity may be assumed. The equivalence of interviewer judgments across groups is consistent with the assumption of objectivity and lack of bias towards one group or the other. This objectivity is crucial since much of the information in this monograph depends on it. At the same time, assuming that the scale is valid, the lack of group differences is an indication that preschool effects are not apparent during the brief observation permitted by an interview.

Interviewers reported that experimental-group youth interviews took place under less satisfactory environmental conditions than did control-group youth interviews (5.0 vs. 5.8 on a 7-point scale, p = .045). It is unlikely that this difference affected the youth interview data in any significant way.

Summary of the Design

The Perry Preschool Project was conducted in Ypsilanti, Michigan with children born each year between 1958 and 1962. These 123 children, all black, were selected on the basis of their parents' low educational attainment and low occupational status and their own initially low cognitive ability—predictors of later academic difficulties. Each year children were assigned to the experimental group or the control group so as to equate the groups on initial cognitive ability, sex ratio, and socioeconomic status. These two groups were equivalent on almost all socioeconomic characteristics of families at project entry and when measured again 11 years later. One group difference, in mothers' employment, appeared at project entry but not later.

Children in the experimental group attended a group preschool program 12½ hours a week and, with their mothers, were visited at home 1½ hours a week—one school year for Wave Zero, two school years for Waves One through Four. The goal of the program was to contribute to the intellectual development and education of each child.

---

*For this scale the alpha coefficient was .894. The alpha coefficient is a measure of how well different items on a scale are measuring the same thing for the respondents in question (see Cronbach, Gleser, Nanda, & Rajaratnam, 1970).

The data reported in this monograph were collected from or about children between ages 3 and 15. There were 48 measures in all—IQ tests, school achievement tests, child rating scales, parent and youth interviews, and school records. There has been almost no absolute attrition of subjects in the sample, with a median rate of missing data of only 5 percent. On the age 14 tests and the age 15 interviews, there was almost no evidence of differential attrition across groups. Interviewers were assigned equally to groups, and groups did not differ in how interviewers rated their members during the interview sessions.

III. Preschool Effects on School Performance and Experience

The Perry Preschool Project used an experimental design—children assigned to experimental and control groups—to discover the long-term effects of preschool education on the participating children. There are compelling reasons to believe that group differences found in this study were actually caused by preschool education.

The analytic framework presented in chapter 1 indicated that preschool education enhanced the school performance and experience of disadvantaged children by improving their cognitive ability at school entry, which led to a heightening of their commitment to schooling, improvements in their school achievement, and reinforcement of a more success-oriented student role by teachers, peers, and parents. The evidence provided by the Perry Preschool study through age 15 fits well with this analytic framework. The evidence is reported in detail in this chapter. It may be summarized as follows.

Improvement in the *cognitive ability at school entry* of children who attended preschool is indicated by their increased IQs during kindergarten and first grade.* Greater *commitment to schooling* is evidenced by more highly rated elementary school motivation, by a higher value placed on schooling by teenagers, and by several other aspects of school commitment. Improved *school achievement* for these children is shown by generally higher achievement test scores during elementary school and distinctly higher scores at eighth grade (age 14) than scores for control group children. *Reinforcement of the student role* is indicated by more highly rated social development in elementary school, fewer years spent in special education, and greater satisfaction and higher aspirations expressed by parents with respect to the schooling of their children.

Effects on Cognitive Ability at School Entry

As shown in figure 2, preschool education improved children's cognitive ability during preschool, kindergarten, and first grade. The best evidence for this comes from comparisons between IQs of the experimental group and the control group, since it might reasonably be assumed that the control group pattern would also have obtained in the experimental group had there been no intervention. The experimental group exceeded the control group by 12 IQ points after one and again after two years of preschool, by 6 points at the end of kindergarten, and by 5 points at the end of first grade (age 7). Contrary to earlier expectations, IQs of the experimental group and the control group were equivalent by the end of second grade and thereafter. At eighth grade (age 14), the Wechsler Intelligence Scale for Children was given instead of the Stanford-Binet because the former was judged to be more suitable for older children and provided subtest scores**as well as a total IQ. Regrettably, no group differences were found in verbal IQ, performance IQ, or any of the subtests.

The average IQ of the control group rose 9 points from age 3 to age 7, then dropped 6 points by age 14. A part of the initial rise in IQ (we estimate about 5 points) may be dismissed as "regression toward the mean," an upward drift of

---

*A statement of preschool effect or group difference is made when the probability of chance occurrence of that group difference was less than 1 in 10 (that is, $p < .100$), with exact, two-tailed p values appearing in the tables.

**The WISC has five verbal subtests—general information, general comprehension, arithmetic, similarities, and vocabulary; and five performance subtests—picture completion, picture arrangement, block design, object assembly, and coding.

32

FIGURE 2 COGNITIVE ABILITY BY GROUP OVER TIME[a]

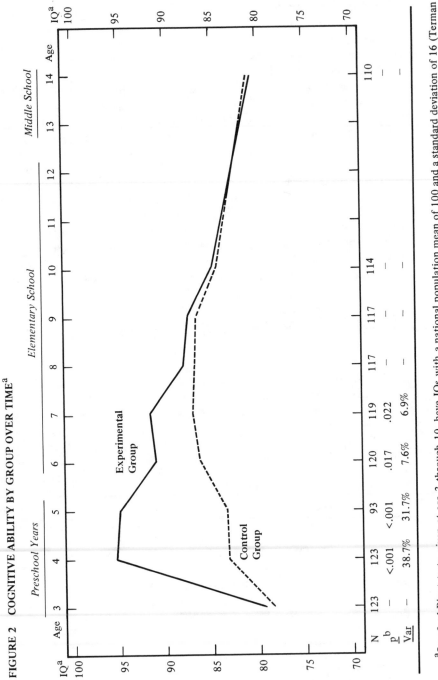

[a]Stanford-Binet tests, given at age 3 through 10, have IQs with a national population mean of 100 and a standard deviation of 16 (Terman & Merrill, 1960). WISC tests, given at age 14, have IQs with a national population mean of 100 and a standard deviation of 15 (Wechsler, 1949). The a_t, an index of consistency over time for these tests, was .921.

[b]p reported if less than .10, followed by the percent of variance accounted for by group membership.

scores that can be expected when a sample of children is chosen on the basis of low scores (Campbell & Erlebacher, 1975). However, it appears that the control group also experienced real shifts in cognitive ability over time, what is here referred to as "systematic change."

Systematic change over time in cognitive ability is almost certainly due to environmental influence. In this study, the control-group IQ rose 4 points from age 3 to age 7 (over and above the 5 points attributed to regression toward the mean), then dropped 6 points by age 14. The experimental-group IQ rose an additional 12 points, then dropped back to the level of the control group. One way to explain the rises in cognitive ability is to say that they are the result of the child's introduction to a more cognitively stimulating environment, that is, an environment in which there is greater opportunity for effective interaction between the child and the environment. Thus we are characterizing the preschool environment as *highly* stimulating cognitively over its two-year duration (enough to result in 12 additional IQ points); and we are characterizing the early elementary school environment as mildly stimulating cognitively (enough for 4 IQ points in the control group) over about the same length of time, that is, during kindergarten and first grade. A similar hypothesis was termed the "freshman effect" by Bloom (1964), thereby emphasizing its transient nature.

Of greater concern is the 6-point drop in the IQ of both groups during the later years of elementary school. If this drop represents a true decrease in cognitive ability, our hypothesis about cognitively stimulating environments may be applied in reverse, suggesting that the later elementary school environments of these children were lacking in effective cognitive stimulation. This lack of effective cognitive stimulation might apply to the later school environment as a whole. Or it might apply only to these children, who as a group tended to have low academic ability—their teachers might have given up on them; they may have given up on themselves as students.

The notion of a "fall" in cognitive ability is really a shorthand way of making a more complex point. If one considers the raw scores, items answered correctly, on the Stanford-Binet test, both the experimental group and the control group increased every year without exception. In other words, their cognitive ability as measured by IQ tests improved every year. But the expectations implied in the test increased at a faster rate. IQ is a ratio which compares a raw score to the raw scores of other children of a given age who took the test, most of whom did not face the same disadvantages as the Perry children. Hence a "fall" in IQ actually meant that their cognitive ability was increasing less rapidly than that of their age-mates.

According to our interpretation, the significance of the improvement in cognitive ability due to preschool was its effect on the way in which the child was introduced to the social system of the school. In this study, the average child who attended preschool went to kindergarten with a functioning IQ of 95; the average child who did not attend preschool went to kindergarten with a functioning IQ of 84. Since IQ tests are designed primarily to correlate highly with school success, it is no surprise that, for 5- and 6-year-olds, the test bears a strong resemblance to the tasks they are called upon to do in kindergarten and first grade. Hence a higher IQ at school entry indicates greater cognitive ability, which is also manifested in more highly successful performance of the scholastic tasks assigned in kindergarten and first grade. The child's initial orientation towards school tasks would then be solidified by a greater commitment to schooling and by adoption of a student role consistent with school success.

Effects on Commitment to Schooling

Within the domain of commitment to schooling, children who had preschool education showed increased motivation during elementary school. At age 15, these children placed a higher value on schooling, had higher aspirations for college, showed greater willingness to talk to parents about school, spent more time on homework, and had a higher self-rating of school ability than the control group.

Elementary-School Motivation and Potential

As shown in table 7, children in the experimental group were rated more highly in school motivation by their elementary school teachers (kindergarten, first, second, and third grades). A similar, though statistically nonsignificant, trend obtained for school potential rated in the same way. The finding on school motivation is evidence of greater commitment to schooling during the elementary school years by children who had had preschool education. Also, the high internal consistency across these repeated measures constitutes evidence that children's positions in a success flow are regarded by the series of elementary school teachers with remarkable consistency.

Value Placed on Schooling at Age 15

Youths who had attended preschool placed a greater value on schooling when they were 15 years old. Value placed on schooling was measured with a 7-item scale which contrasted the value of schooling in terms of learning and personal worth with experience outside of school. The scale was also used in the Youth in Transition Study (Bachman, O'Malley, & Johnston, 1978). While the overall result combined with a modest internal consistency in the scale suggests that the items tended to be in agreement with the overall result, the item which best discriminated between groups was: "All people should have at least a high school education." In the experimental group, 97 percent of the youths agreed with the statement pretty much or very much, while in the control group only 84 percent of the youths agreed with the statement to that extent.

Other Aspects of School Commitment at Age 15

Table 8 lists findings for items from the youth interview (one item from the concurrent parent interview) which bear on youths' commitment to schooling. The first two items have to do with thoughts about one's educational future. Children who attended preschool were more likely to have thought of going to college, but were no more certain about their own high school graduation than the control group. The question on thoughts about college may be regarded as a question about educational aspirations, a topic whose importance has been emphasized by Turner (1964). The lack of a group difference concerning certainty about high school graduation suggests that this question concerns educational expectations without reference to aspirations. These two items could be taken to indicate that preschool heightens the discrepancy between one's aspirations and what one can expect to occur, a condition which leads to increased deviance according to the "strain" theory of Cloward and Ohlin (1961). However, that does not seem to be the case in this study.

TABLE 7   SCHOOL COMMITMENT OF YOUTHS BY GROUP

Variable	Group[a]	Percentage of Group Reporting					p[b]	Var

YOUTH AGES 6-9, RATINGS BY TEACHERS[c]
(N = 95)

School motivation

9 items scored 9-45; a_t[d]=.829
e.g., shows initiative, alert and
interested in schoolwork, motivated
toward academic performance

		Scoring Range: 9-16	17-24	25-31	32-38	39-45		
		% within range:						
	Exp	4	31	33	22	11		
	Ctl	10	41	25	25	0	.087	4.2%

School potential

3 items scored 3-21, a_t=.839
e.g., degree of imagination and creativity,
academic readiness, predicted future
academic success

		Scoring Range: 3-9	10-13	14-17	18-21		
		% within range:					
	Exp	32	36	24	8		
	Ctl	47	22	27	4	—	

YOUTH AGE 15, SELF-RATINGS
(N = 99)

Value placed on schooling

7 items scored 7-28; a = .634

		Scoring Range: 12-19	20-22	23-25	26-28		
		% within range:					
	Exp	9	16	36	39		
	Ctl	15	24	34	28	.024	5.3%

Items:	**Agree with statement:**	**Not at all**	**A little**	**Pretty much**	**Very much**		
All people should have at least a high school education.	Exp	0	2	11	86		
	Ctl	6	11	11	73	.066	3.4%
Even if I could get a very good job at present, I'd still choose to stay in school and get my education.	Exp	0	9	9	82		
	Ctl	0	9	18	73	—	
I think school is important not only for the practical value, but because learning itself is very worthwhile.	Exp	0	16	16	68		
	Ctl	4	13	20	64	—	
A real education comes from things you learn in school and not from your own experiences.[e]	Exp	7	16	41	36		
	Ctl	22	18	26	35	—	
I can satisfy my curiosity better by the things I learn here at school than by the things I learn outside of school.	Exp	11	9	46	34		
	Ctl	16	15	33	36	—	
I feel I can learn more here at school than I can from a very good job.[e]	Exp	9	9	18	64		
	Ctl	9	17	28	46	—	
I feel the things I do outside of school waste my time more than the things I do at school.[e]	Exp	7	5	16	73		
	Ctl	6	4	36	55	—	

[a]Exp = experimental, ctl = control.

[b]The two-tailed p value, based on the Mann-Whitney U test, was reported if less than .100, followed by the percent of variance accounted for by group membership.

[c]Scores were averaged across at least 3 of 4 measures at kindergarten, first, second, and third grades.

[d]a_t is the alpha coefficient for the total score, treating reported measures as items; it is an index of consistency of measurement over time.

[e]Phrasing was modified in this report to make scoring in the same direction across all items on the scale.

TABLE 8   ASPECTS OF SCHOOL COMMITMENT BY GROUP

Item[a]	Category	Percentage of Experimental Group	Control Group	p[b]	Var
Have you ever thought of going to college?	yes	77	60	.077	3.3%
	no	23	40		
How certain are you that you actually will graduate?	certain	48	51	—	
	fairly certain	30	28		
	less certain	14	8		
	chances slim	9	13		
Parent: How willing is your child to talk about what s/he is doing in school?	enjoys it	65	33	.004	8.7%
	talks when asked	29	56		
	doesn't like to	2	7		
	refuses	4	4		
How satisfied are you with the way you're actually doing in school?	very	27	31	—	
	quite	43	26		
	somewhat	21	26		
	not very	7	15		
	not at all	2	4		
Does your schoolwork require preparation by you at home?	yes	68	40	.006	7.9%
	no	32	60		
How many days a week do you spend time outside of school in preparation for classes?	0	39	62	.044	6.1%
	1-2	30	20		
	3-4	11	9		
	5-6	20	9		
Compared with others in your grade, how do you rate yourself in school ability?	much more	9	4	.009	7.1%
	more	23	15		
	a little more	55	40		
	a little less	5	26		
	less	5	6		
	much less	5	9		
Compared with others in your grade, how do you rate yourself in how smart you are?	much more	5	9	—	
	more	23	15		
	a little more	52	47		
	less[c]	20	30		
What is the average grade you got in your classes last year?	A	14	11	—	
	B	34	35		
	C	52	46		
	D	0	7		
	F	0	2		

[a] N = 99 for youth items, 102 for the parent item.

[b] The two-tailed p value, based on the Mann-Whitney U test or the chi-square test (for dichotomous variables), was reported if less than .100, followed by the percent of variance accounted for by group membership.

[c] "Less" combines "a little less," "less," and "much less."

Parents reported that youths who had attended preschool were in more cases willing to talk about what they were doing in school; 65 percent of the experimental group said they enjoyed talking about school, while only 33 percent of the control group said they enjoyed it. This greater willingness might conceivably have been due to a better parent-youth relationship, with more communication in all areas; but there were no broader differences between groups in parent-youth relationship (see table 15). Greater willingness to talk about school may indicate that youths who had attended preschool were more strongly committed to their school experiences and more willing to take credit for them.

Groups did not differ in youths' satisfaction with their own school performance. It cannot be determined from this item whether this equivalence in satisfaction also represents equivalence in standards for satisfaction.

Findings on the next two items indicated that youths who had attended preschool were more likely to do homework and spent more time doing it. We have chosen to regard homework primarily as evidence of commitment to schooling, since actually doing homework probably depends more on student motivation than on teacher assignments. However, it is also possible that, because of various tracking and grouping procedures, children in the control group were actually assigned less homework. Whichever interpretation is valid, or if both interpretations are valid, the findings constitute interesting evidence of the long-term impact of preschool education.

On self-ratings of one's position compared to peers, youths who had attended preschool rated themselves higher on school ability but not on "how smart you are." It is interesting to note that these responses differentiated between competence in the school setting and a more general intellectual competence.

There were no group differences in average grade reported.

Effects on School Achievement

Preschool education contributed to increased school achievement during the years of elementary and middle school, as indicated in figure 3. Differences favoring preschool were between 5 and 7 percent of items passed* from age 7 to age 10, but dropped to 2 percent at age 11. At age 14, there was a highly significant difference of 8 percent of items passed in favor of children who attended preschool. Reading, arithmetic, and language achievement subtest results—shown in figures 3A, 3B, and 3C—followed a similar pattern over time.

Group distributions on the age 14 achievement test, depicted in figure 4, show the importance of such an overall difference to individual students. The distribution for the control group is concentrated below 40 percent, peaking at about 25 percent. The distribution for the experimental group has a broader spread than the control group, with a sizable portion above 40 percent and therefore above most of the control group.

Group comparisons on subtests of the age 14 achievement test are presented in figure 5. The subtest results were consistent with the overall test result, except for the subtest of reading comprehension, which failed to register a

---

*Percentage of items passed was selected over other metrics, such as grade equivalents, percentiles, and raw scores, because it focuses attention on the comparison between groups while maintaining some degree of comparability over time.

38

FIGURE 3   TOTAL SCHOOL ACHIEVEMENT BY GROUP OVER TIME[a]

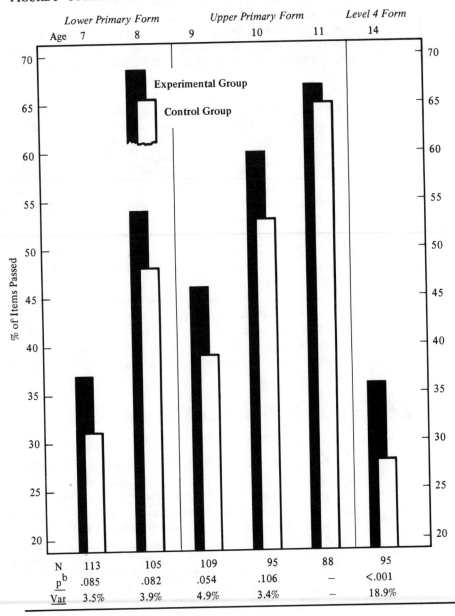

N	113	105	109	95	88	95
p^b	.085	.082	.054	.106	–	<.001
Var	3.5%	3.9%	4.9%	3.4%	–	18.9%

[a]California Achievement Tests (Tiegs & Clark, 1963, 1970). The a_t, an index of the consistency of measurement over time, was .953. The a for the age 14 test (the only one for which a was assessed) was .966.

[b]p is reported if less than .10, followed by the percent of variance accounted for by group membership.

FIGURE 3A   READING ACHIEVEMENT BY GROUP OVER TIME

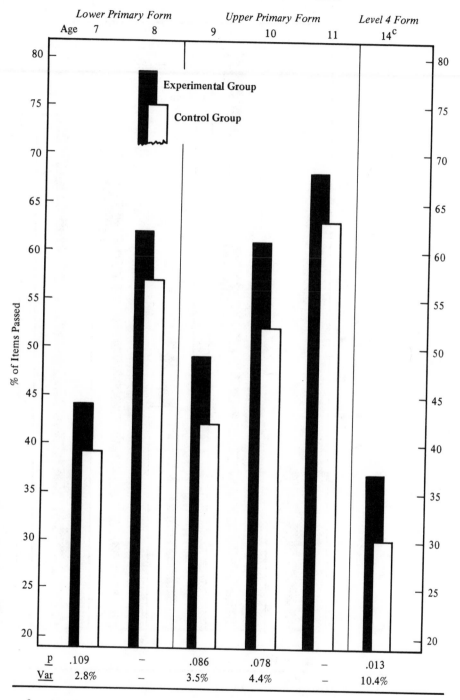

| | p | .109 | — | .086 | .078 | — | .013 |
| | Var | 2.8% | — | 3.5% | 4.4% | — | 10.4% |

[c] a = .879

40

FIGURE 3B   ARITHMETIC ACHIEVEMENT BY GROUP OVER TIME

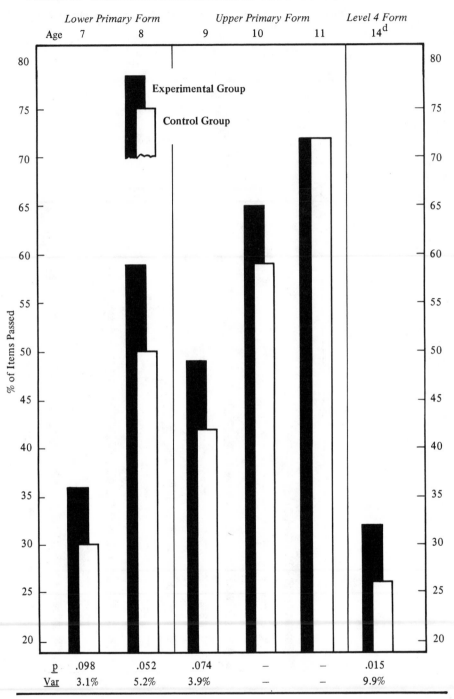

	Age 7	8	9	10	11	14[d]
p	.098	.052	.074	–	–	.015
Var	3.1%	5.2%	3.9%	–	–	9.9%

[d] a = .911

FIGURE 3C LANGUAGE ACHIEVEMENT BY GROUP OVER TIME

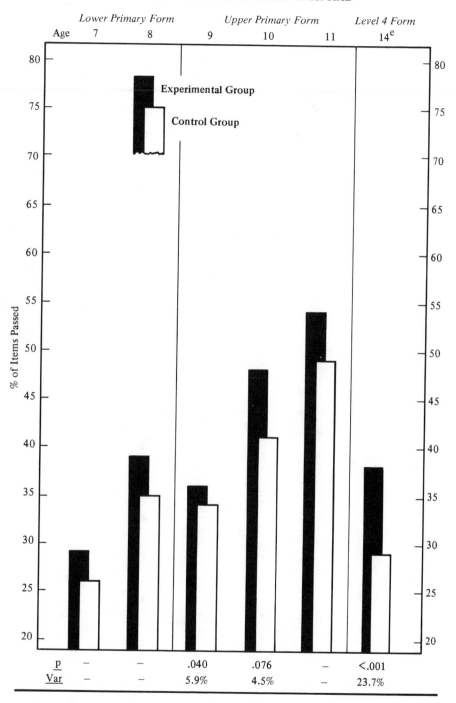

		Age	7	8	9	10	11	14^e

Lower Primary Form   Upper Primary Form   Level 4 Form

% of Items Passed

Experimental Group

Control Group

p	–	–	.040	.076	–	<.001
Var	–	–	5.9%	4.5%	–	23.7%

^{e} **a** = .917

42

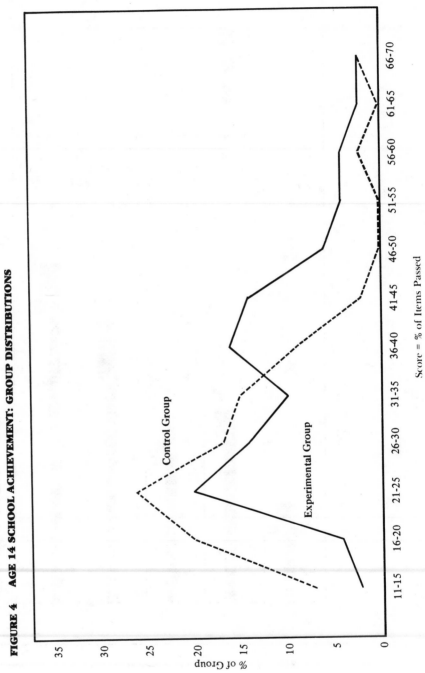

FIGURE 4   AGE 14 SCHOOL ACHIEVEMENT: GROUP DISTRIBUTIONS

FIGURE 5   AGE 14 SCHOOL ACHIEVEMENT SUBTESTS BY GROUP[a]

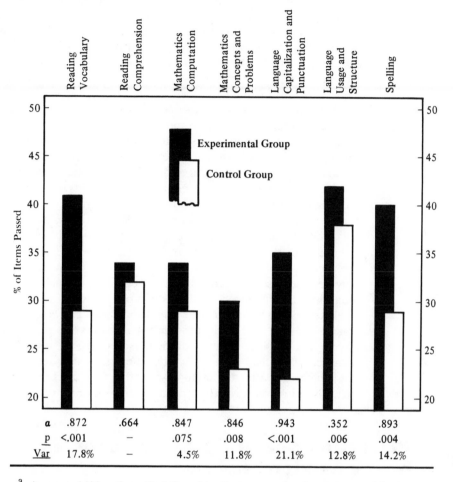

	Reading Vocabulary	Reading Comprehension	Mathematics Computation	Mathematics Concepts and Problems	Language Capitalization and Punctuation	Language Usage and Structure	Spelling
a	.872	.664	.847	.846	.943	.352	.893
p	<.001	–	.075	.008	<.001	.006	.004
Var	17.8%	–	4.5%	11.8%	21.1%	12.8%	14.2%

[a] p is reported if less than .10, followed by the percent of variance accounted for by group membership.

group difference. One factor in this lack of a group difference may have been the subtest's relatively low internal consistency.* On the other hand, there was a group difference on the subtest of language usage and structure, a subtest with an even lower level of internal consistency. The lack of consistency within this subtest is of some interest as it bears on the debate about the use of standard English in the schools by minority-group members (Cazden, Baratz, Labov, & Palmer, 1973). One series of items on the subtest asks the respondent to find the errors in a text in terms of standard English. Apparently, the interpretation of these items by the respondents was extremely variable.

A closer examination of the age 14 achievement test suggests that preschool education led not only to improved school achievement but also to greater *persistence* in carrying out these academic tasks. For each item on the test, the test-takers have three alternatives: (1) respond correctly, (2) respond incorrectly, or (3) do not respond at all. The achievement score is based on the number of correct responses—at age 14, 36 percent for the experimental group

---

*The extent to which all the items measured the same thing; represented by the alpha coefficient.

and 28 percent for the control group. Combining correct and incorrect responses produces the number of items attempted—which we are viewing as evidence of task persistence. At age 14 the experimental group attempted 89 percent of the items, while the control group attempted 82 percent. Or, viewed another way, the nonresponse rate was 11 percent in the experimental group and 18 percent in the control group ($p = .004$). Since achievement tests represent academic learning, task persistence is not alone sufficient to explain higher test scores. But task persistence, direct evidence of commitment to achievement, surely contributes to higher achievement; and higher achievement surely contributes to greater commitment and persistence.

Further light is shed on this matter by a comparison of the procedures for administration of the IQ test and the achievement test. It is puzzling that a large group difference appeared at age 14 on the achievement test, but not on the IQ test. While both kinds of tests were administered by trained testers employed by the High/Scope Foundation, IQ tests were given individually, while the achievement tests were given in groups. The IQ testers personally maintained the attention and persistence of the test-takers—waiting for each response, writing it down, and minimizing the number of items presented which the test-takers could not answer correctly. In contrast, the achievement testers provided only general test instructions at the beginning of each section of the test, monitored completion of the items in a passive way, and made no attempt to shield test-takers from items they could not answer correctly. Thus achievement test performance, but not IQ test performance, was dependent on the degree of attention and task persistence of the person taking the test. We conclude that teenagers who had preschool education showed greater persistence on academic tasks without continuous attention from teachers. It may be assumed that this condition was fairly typical in their classrooms.

Effects on Social Reinforcement of the Student Role

Children who received preschool education required and received fewer years of special education services during the course of their schooling. Their social development was enhanced during their elementary school years. When they were teenagers, their parents were better satisfied with their school performance and had higher aspirations for their educational attainment. Their parents were less frequently called in to talk to their teachers about their children. While, in retrospect, coverage of the domain of role reinforcement from teachers, peers, and parents was far from complete, some of the most important variables in the study fit into this domain. Their importance comes both from their economic implications and from their profound impact on the lives and experiences of children.

Reinforcement from Teachers: Special Education

As this report was being prepared, the complete school records of all members of the sample were examined, from kindergarten through twelfth grade. As shown in figure 6, by the end of high school 39 percent of the control group had received special education services for one year or more, compared with only 19 percent of the experimental group.

FIGURE 6   YEARS IN SPECIAL EDUCATION BY GROUP

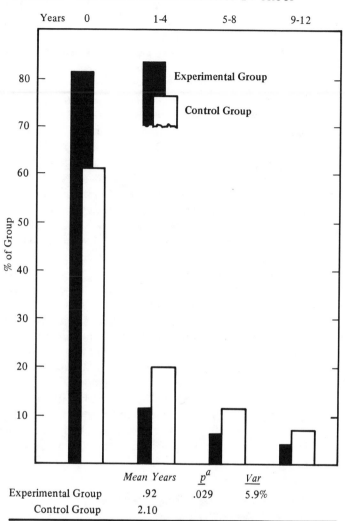

$^a\underline{p}$ is followed by the percent of variance accounted for by group membership.

The procedure for certifying a child as handicapped and in need of special education services usually began with the classroom teacher. The teacher recommended that a child be diagnosed by a special education official. This official took into account the teacher's opinions about the child's classroom behavior and potential as well as the child's performance on various tests, particularly tests of cognitive ability. These children were in almost all cases diagnosed prior to adoption of the formal procedures mandated by the Education of All Handicapped Children Act of 1975.

The 30 percent of the sample who were diagnosed as handicapped were further analyzed for type of handicap and onset and duration of special education services. The groups did not differ on any of these variables. Of the 37 children in the sample judged to be handicapped, it was found that 25 were classified as educable mentally retarded (EMR), not surprising in light of their initial selection on this criterion; 19 were classified as EMR only, 4 began as EMR and

46

were later classified as learning disabled (LD), a milder category, and 2 were doubly classified as EMR and emotionally impaired (EI). Of the remainder, 4 were classified as EI only, 2 as LD only, and 2 as simultaneously EI and LD. Type of handicap was not recorded for 5 children who were classified as handicapped.

About two-thirds of those classified as handicapped were classified as such during elementary school—5 children in grades 1 or 2, 13 in grades 3 or 4, and 6 in grades 5 or 6. The rest of the handicap classifications were concentrated in the middle-school years—9 in grades 7 or 8, 3 in grades 9 or 10, and 1 in grade 11. The average time spent receiving special education services, for children classified as handicapped, was 5.3 years.

There were no group differences in the number of years retained in grade; as of eighth grade the sample as a whole averaged .13 years retained in grade. In a previous monograph (Weikart, Bond, & McNeil, 1978), grade retentions were combined with special education placements and regular placements into an overall measure of school success. But with the passage of time it has become clear that grade retentions were relatively inconsequential for this sample of children. In fact, David Weikart, when he was with the Ypsilanti Public School System (1957-1970), sought to institute a policy of minimal use of grade retention; apparently he was successful.

Special education placement fits into our conceptual framework as a type of reinforcement of the child's student role by teachers and other school personnel. A child who needs special education services certainly ought to receive them, but an unfortunate consequence of this procedure is that the child is labeled as having a more restricted potential and may in fact be dealt with in such a way as to maintain this restricted potential.

Special education placement and grade retention are merely the formal and visible tracking procedures in the school. Rist (1970) observed a variety of grouping procedures leading to differential treatment, in classrooms similar to the ones these children attended. Special education placement may have been but the tip of an iceberg, with each child being placed in an almost permanent category defining a level of success as early as the first few days of school.

Reinforcement from Peers: Social Development

While our evidence on peer reinforcement of the child's student role is quite limited, it was found that elementary school teachers rated children who attended preschool as better developed socially. This scale consisted of three items: social relationships with classmates, relationship with teacher, and level of curiosity shown.* No group differences were found for other teacher ratings of the child's social behavior in elementary school—emotional adjustment, social-emotional state, or independence from teacher.

Reinforcement from Parents: Satisfaction and Aspirations

Table 9 portrays findings for variables concerning the parent's relation to the child's schooling.

During elementary school, teachers rated the mother's participation in her child's schooling at the same level for the experimental group and the control group.

*a_t = .713, p = .050, Var = 5.3%

TABLE 9 PARENTS' RELATION TO YOUTH'S SCHOOLING BY GROUP

Variable	Category	Percentage of		p^a	Var
		Experimental Group	Control Group		
YOUTH AGES 6-9, ASKED OF TEACHER:	**Scoring Range:**				
Participation by mother (N = 105)	12-14	10	13	—
2 items scored 2-14; $a_t{}^b$ = .795	9-11	40	35		
mother's degree of cooperation,	6-8	24	24		
prediction of mother's future	2-5	26	28		
school relationship					
YOUTH AGE 15, ASKED OF PARENT: (N = 102)					
Has your child done as well in	yes	51	28	.014	9.9%
school as you would have liked?	no	45	70		
	no opinion[c]	4	2		
How much schooling would you	college degree	50	34	.027	5.3%
hope your child would get?	some college	27	26		
	high school	15	34		
	as far as s/he wants[c]	8	6		
How far do you think s/he	college degree	23	16	—	
will actually go in school?	some college	21	17		
	high school	44	55		
	some high school	10	13		
	as far as s/he wants[c]	2	0		
Have you done anything to help	yes	78	73	—	
your child do well in school?	no	23	27		
How useful do you think that	very useful	56	60	—	
parent-teacher conferences are?	useful	27	23		
	somewhat useful	15	13		
	not at all useful	2	4		
Over the years how often have	always	42	61	.030	4.7%
you gone to parent-teacher	most of the time	29	22		
conferences when *invited* by	sometimes	10	9		
one of your child's teachers?	once in a while	6	7		
	never	13	0		
How often have you gotten in	often	19	25	—	
touch with teachers *on your own*	occasionally	51	47		
to talk about your child's	never	30	28		
progress?					
YOUTH AGE 15, ASKED OF YOUTH: (N = 99)					
Do your parents talk with your	yes	52	79	.005	13.4%
teacher about your schoolwork?	no	48	21		
How much do your parents attend	very much	9	15	—	
school activities or functions?	pretty much	14	26		
	a little	48	38		
	not at all	30	22		

[a] The two-tailed p value, based on the Mann-Whitney U test or the chi-square test (for dichotomous variables), was reported if less than .100, followed by the percent of variance accounted for by group membership.

[b] a_t is an index of the consistency of measurement over time.

[c] Category not included in the analysis.

When their children were 15 years old, over half of the experimental-group parents expressed satisfaction with the school performance of their children, while only a little more than one fourth of the control-group parents did so. There is no reason to assume that parents differed by group in what was required to satisfy them. On the other hand, there is considerable evidence that experimental-group children were doing better in school than control-group children and were more willing to communicate this fact to their parents.

The next two items listed, on parents' educational aspirations and expectations for their children, are in agreement with the findings for youths' responses to these questions: higher *aspirations* in the experimental group, but equivalent *expectations* by both groups. An explanation for this finding may be that aspirations are based mainly on school performance, while expectations are tempered by concern about the family's ability to afford the costs of higher education.

The remaining series of items bear on the issue of how the parent actually related to teachers and the school. In items not on the table, almost all the parents agreed that parents should be involved in what goes on in school (98 percent), that education was very important (97 percent), and that they were very concerned about what goes on in school (83 percent). Three out of four parents said they had done things to help their child do well in school and agreed that parent-teacher conferences were useful. About two out of three parents had at least occasionally taken the initiative to talk to teachers about their child's progress. According to youths, the majority of parents attended school activities "a little." There were no group differences on any of these variables.

However, according to youths, over three out of four control-group parents talked with teachers about their schoolwork, while this was the case for only about half of the experimental-group parents. This finding is both corroborated and refined by the additional finding that control-group parents reported a greater frequency of going to parent-teacher conferences at the invitation of the teacher. On first impression, the apparent finding that parents whose children attended preschool were less involved in their children's education seems inconsistent with all the other findings of this study. However, a more reasonable way to view these data is that the increased teacher-parent contact in the control group was a reaction to a greater number of school-related problems and difficulties with schoolwork. It seems likely that control-group parents were more often *called in* by teachers to discuss their children's schoolwork. While parental involvement in schools is certainly valuable in itself, this particular form of involvement may well have been both an expression and a reinforcement of a school role of the child oriented towards failure or deviance.

IV. Preschool Effects on Deviance and Social Patterns

The analytic framework in chapter 1 indicated that, by its enhancement of the schooling of disadvantaged children, preschool education led to a decrease in their deviant behavior and an increase in their adult success. Deviant behavior was assessed through school conduct and delinquent behavior. Age 15 was too early to assess the types of adult success implied, such as educational attainment and employment patterns, although teenage employment was considered a relevant indicator.

The Perry Preschool study through age 15 provides the following evidence in these domains. Decreased *deviant behavior at school* by children who had attended preschool is indicated by more favorably rated classroom conduct and personal behavior during elementary school and by teenagers' reports of being kept after school less often.* Decreased *delinquent behavior* is shown by lower scores for total self-reported delinquent behavior and serious delinquent behavior, specifically in the serious categories of taking something from a person by force and damaging institutional property. A possible trend towards future *employment success* is shown by the fact that 29 percent of teenagers who had attended preschool currently had a job, compared with only 16 percent of teenagers in the control group.

Our analytic framework focused on schooling and its *direct* outcomes, thereby excluding alternative or supplementary paths which might also have been affected by preschool education. Some variables outside the analytic framework were assessed at age 15, though it is more appropriate to say that group differences on these variables were *hoped for* rather than expected, for a variety of reasons. *Self-concept,* while logically related to school success and commitment, is seldom measured in a precise, reliable, and valid way. The *general parent-youth relationship* is only tangentially related to schooling during the teenage years, when the influence of the home competes with that of peers and the "media." The *social patterns and use of leisure time by youths,* except for deviant behavior, are not directly related to school success, and thus were outside the major paths affected by preschool education. The same is true of *parents' use of time.*

No group differences of consequence were found on any of these variables. Findings are briefly presented here to fill out the picture of the lives of these teenagers and their families. These findings of no group differences highlight the importance of concentrating upon schooling and its direct outcomes in an analytic framework for the longitudinal study of early educational intervention.

Effects on Deviant Behavior in School

As indicated in table 10, preschool education led to improved classroom conduct and improved personal behavior, as rated by elementary school teachers. Combined, these two factors consisted of 18 categories of deviant classroom behavior. The categories were originally developed by Vinter et al. (1966) to assess the "pre-delinquent" behavior of students. There was an effort made to insure their validity and significance beyond the classroom, that is, in the community.

---

*As in previous chapters, a statement of preschool effect or group difference is made when the probability of chance occurrence was less than .100, with the exact *p* values appearing in the tables.

Table 10 also shows that preschool education had no apparent effect on the school conduct of teenagers. However, preschool did lead to a reduction in the frequency of being kept after class, with 14 percent of the experimental group reporting that they were kept after school sometimes, often, or almost always, and 27 percent of the control group reporting that they were kept after school that frequently. As one looks over the categories of school conduct assessed at age 15, one wonders if youths were kept after school for reasons more serious than we were able to ascertain using these categories of school conduct.

TABLE 10　SCHOOL CONDUCT BY GROUP

Variable	Category	Percentage of Experimental Group	Control Group	p^a	Var
YOUTH AGES 6-9, RATINGS BY TEACHERS[b] (N = 95)					
Classroom conduct	Scoring Range:				
12 items scored 12-60; a_t^c = .762	51-60[d]	22	4	.061	3.7%
e.g., does not blame others for	41-50	48	48		
trouble, is not resistant to teacher,	31-40	24	41		
does not attempt to manipulate adults.[d]	21-30	7	10		
Personal behavior	Scoring Range:				
6 items scored 6-30; a_t = .754	26-30[d]	42	29	.060	3.8%
e.g., lack of absences or truances,	21-25	49	57		
appropriate personal appearance, lack of lying or cheating.[d]	15-20	9	14		
YOUTH AGE 15, SELF-RATINGS (N = 99)					
School conduct	Scoring Range:				
9 items scored 5-45; a = .747	30-36[d]	30	23	—	
e.g., not skipping class, not	22-29	48	46		
coming to class late or unprepared,	14-21	20	25		
not threatening teachers, not cheating on tests, not copying assignments.[d]	10-13	3	2		
How often are you kept after school?	almost always	0	6	.078	3.2%
	often	5	4		
	sometimes	9	17		
	seldom	18	22		
	never	68	52		

[a] The two-tailed p value, based on the Mann-Whitney U test, was reported if less than .100, followed by the percent of variance accounted for by group membership.

[b] Scale scores were averaged across at least 3 of 4 measures at kindergarten, first grade, second grade and third grade.

[c] a_t is an index of the consistency of measurement over time.

[d] Item phrasing and scores for conduct are expressed positively, so that a higher score means better conduct.

Effects on Delinquent Behavior

Preschool education led to a decrease in teenagers' delinquent behavior; we postulate that it did so by strengthening their bonds to schooling. Figure 7 portrays the distributions of total self-reported delinquent behavior* in the experimental group and in the control group. Wolfgang, Figlio, and Sellin (1972), in their landmark study of delinquency, divided youths into non-offenders, one-time offenders, multiple offenders, and chronic offenders (five or more offenses). In these terms, the most striking differences in the distribution were that (1) taking non-offenders and one-time offenders as one combined category, the experimental group had 43 percent of its members in that category, while the control group had only 25 percent; and (2) the experimental group had 36 percent of its members in the category of chronic offenders with five or more offenses, while the control group had 52 percent.

FIGURE 7   SELF-REPORTED DELINQUENT BEHAVIOR BY GROUP

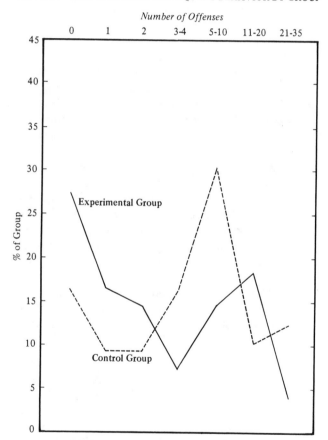

The experimental group scored less than the control group, median test, p = .022, Var = 5.4%.

---

*In a technique suggested by Gold (see Berger, Crowley, Gold, & Gray, 1975, Note 6), self-reported delinquent behavior which subjects regarded as trivial was excluded from further data analysis. Examples of such behavior would be fighting or petty stealing from a sibling during childhood.

54

In a second analysis of these data, the experimental group was found to score lower than the control group on a *serious delinquency* scale (median test, p = .048, *Var* = 4.0 percent). The scale, modeled after the Sellin-Wolfgang scale (Sellin & Wolfgang, 1964), consisted of categories of delinquent behavior which involve violence or the taking of property, weighted as shown in table 11. A score of 0 or 1 was found for 61 percent of the experimental group, but for only 40 percent of the control group. A score of 3 or more was found for 35 percent of the experimental group and 51 percent of the control group.

Table 11 lists outcomes in specific categories of self-reported delinquent behavior, arranged in order of decreasing seriousness. Three categories were found to have statistically significant group differences, all with a lower frequency of delinquent behavior reported by the experimental group: taking something by force from a person, damaging institutional property, and lying about age or identification. Legally, taking something by force from a person would be classified, depending on the seriousness of the offense, as armed robbery, unarmed robbery, or purse-snatching. Damaging institutional property would be classified, again depending on seriousness, as either malicious destruction of property or vandalism. Lying about age or identification would only be illegal in the case of a minor attempting to purchase an intoxicating beverage.

There was a noticeable trend, though not statistically significant, for the control group to report having been caught more often for breaking the law.

Gender differences in delinquent behavior are a key question in the study of delinquency, if only because females have been excluded from so many studies (Cernkovich & Giordano, 1979). Gender differences in self-reported delinquent behavior in this sample (experimental and control groups combined) were not great. There was no difference in total delinquent behavior. Boys had a higher score on the serious delinquent behavior scale (p = .018, *Var* = 5.8 percent), with no serious involvements reported by 31 percent of boys, but 48 percent of girls. Boys also had higher scores for three categories of delinquent behavior: taking by force from a person (14 percent of boys with at least one offense vs. 2 percent of girls, p = .069), group fight (40 percent of boys with at least one offense vs. 14 percent of girls, p = .005), and damaging personal property (30 percent of boys with at least one offense vs. 10 percent of girls, p = .011).

Taking either boys alone or girls alone, the experimental group had lower scores than the control group in total and serious delinquent behavior, although these differences were not statistically significant.

Effects on Teenage Employment

As shown in table 12, teenage employment prior to leaving school is a spare-time activity. Almost two-thirds of the sample had a job at one time or another. There was a noticeable though statistically nonsignificant difference between groups in terms of current employment, with 29 percent of the experimental group and 16 percent of the control group working. Current employment was during the school year. (Summer employment was not assessed.) These jobs paid an average of two dollars an hour, the legal minimum wage in 1975. The average teenager in the sample worked a little over 14 hours a week and had been employed almost a year.

While it is true that teenage employment is a marginal, transitional activity, it is also a real-life expression, with economic implications, of such social virtues as task persistence and commitment to success. The trend for a higher proportion of the experimental group to be currently employed is a hopeful sign that the greater success in schooling induced by preschool education will extend to employment and other kinds of success beyond the classroom.

TABLE 11   TYPES OF SELF-REPORTED DELINQUENT BEHAVIOR BY GROUP

Category (weight in parentheses)	Group[a]	Percentage of Each Group Reporting:					p[b]	Var
		Never	Once	Twice	Occasional	Habitual		
Taking by force from person (3)	Exp	98	2	0	0	0	.034	4.6%
	Ctl	86	7	0	4	4		
Threat of injury (2)	Exp	71	9	7	7	7	—	
	Ctl	60	22	4	9	6		
Purposeful injury (1)	Exp	84	7	2	2	5	—	
	Ctl	82	13	0	4	2		
Hit parent (1)	Exp	98	2	0	0	0	—	
	Ctl	98	2	0	0	0		
Group fight (1)	Exp	73	5	7	5	11	—	
	Ctl	71	11	4	7	7		
Damaged personal property (1)	Exp	75	18	5	2	0	—	
	Ctl	80	9	6	5	0		
Damaged institutional property (1)	Exp	98	2	0	0	0	.033	4.6%
	Ctl	86	6	4	5	0		
Taking personal property (1)	Exp	75	18	2	5	0	—	
	Ctl	73	13	5	2	7		
Taking institutional property (1)	Exp	77	18	0	2	2	—	
	Ctl	78	13	0	2	7		
Other drugs for "kicks" (0)	Exp	93	5	2	0	0	—	
	Ctl	98	2	0	0	0		
Smoked marijuana (0)	Exp	84	5	2	7	2	—	
	Ctl	87	4	2	4	4		
Lie about age or ID (0)	Exp	84	14	0	0	2	.079	3.2%
	Ctl	71	11	6	4	9		
Drinking without permission (0)	Exp	75	2	9	9	5	—	
	Ctl	76	6	0	9	9		
Con (swindle) (0)	Exp	82	4	3	5	6	—	
	Ctl	78	2	6	7	7		
Carried gun or knife (0)	Exp	71	21	2	2	5	—	
	Ctl	73	6	4	6	13		
Ran away (0)	Exp	96	2	2	0	0	—	
	Ctl	87	9	4	0	0		
Caught for breaking law[c]	Exp	84	14	2	0	0	—	
	Ctl	75	13	9	0	4		

[a]Exp = experimental, ctl = control; N = 99.

[b]The two-tailed p value, based on the Mann-Whitney U test, was reported if less than .100, followed by the percent of variance accounted for by group membership.

[c]Not part of either delinquency scale.

TABLE 12   YOUTH EMPLOYMENT BY GROUP

Variable[a]		Experimental Group	Control Group	p[b]	Var
Have you ever had a job?	yes	66%	58%	—	
	no	34%	22%		
Are you working now or	yes	29%	16%	—	
have you worked in the	no	71%	84%		
past two months?					
Present or last job					
Number of cases		17	22		
Pay per hour		$1.87	$2.11	—	
Hours per week		14.2	14.4	—	
Months on job		10.2	11.3	—	

[a]N = 99 for first two variables.

[b]The two-tailed p value, based on the analysis of variance, was reported if less than .100, followed by the percent of variance accounted for by group membership.

General Social Patterns

There were no group differences found among variables classified as general social patterns. Findings for these variables are reported below under the headings *general self-concept, general parent-youth relationship, social patterns of youths, time use by youths,* and *time use by parents.*

General Self-Concept

Findings for aspects of general self-concept, measured by the age 15 youth interview, are shown in table 13. On the scales representing self-confidence, meeting others' expectations, and work ethic, there were slight, though statistically nonsignificant, trends favoring the experimental group. The difficulties of measuring self-concept are well known (for example, Wylie, 1974). The low internal consistencies obtained in this study (indicated by the alpha coefficients for each scale) made it very unlikely that group differences would be found even if they did exist.

General Parent-Youth Relationship

Early intervention, as a kind of childcare program, has sometimes been accused of weakening the family structure and undermining the authority of parents. If such charges were true, the evidence should appear in these variables representing the parent-youth relationship. In fact, there was no evidence to indicate that preschool education had any effect on the parent-youth relationship, except as it influenced the parents' attitudes towards the youth's schooling, as reported in the preceding chapter.

TABLE 13   ASPECTS OF GENERAL SELF-CONCEPT BY GROUP

Variable[a]	Score	Percentage of		p[b]	Var
		Experimental Group	Control Group		
Self-confidence	Scoring Range:				
4 items scored 5-20; a = .424	16-20	42	35	—	
e.g., I am a person of worth vs.	11-15	56	59		
I'm no good	5-10	2	6		
Meeting others' expectations	Scoring Range:				
3 items scored 3-15; a = .424	12-15	33	21	—	
Items: teachers, parents,	8-11	52	62		
friends	3-7	15	12		
Work ethic					
4 items scored 4-8; a = .232					
e.g., Would you rather: have some-	8	7	6	—	
one compliment your work (1) or	7	42	19		
feel you had done your best (2)?	6	26	22		
	5	23	44		
	4	2	9		
Self in control					
4 items scored 4-8; a = .541					
e.g., I have found that what is	8	5	11	—	
going to happen will happen (1)	7	36	34		
or Being just plain lucky has never	6	38	34		
turned out right for me, and I did	5	19	21		
better when I made up my mind to do	4	2	0		
something and did it (2).					

[a] N = 99.

[b] The two-tailed p value, based on the Mann-Whitney U test, was reported if less than .100, followed by the percent of variance accounted for by group membership.

As shown in table 14, there were no group differences in assessment of the quality of parenting, from either the parents' or the youths' point of view. A group difference was found on one item, asked of only one wave of parents (N = 27): "How often do you talk over important decisions with your child?" Experimental-group parents said "always" in 42 percent of the cases, with the control group at 13 percent; experimental-group parents said "seldom" in no cases, with the control group at 20 percent (p = .066). However, this group difference was not corroborated by youths. As a sidelight, comparison of the items common to the two scales revealed that parents viewed the quality of their parenting more favorably than did youths.

With respect to the closeness of parents and youths, there were no group differences. In addition to the data reported in table 14, parent respondents, 96 percent of whom were mothers or other female guardians, reported their closeness to the youths as follows: 68 percent extremely close, 19 percent somewhat close, and 3 percent not very close. In the two-parent families reported in the table (58 percent of the sample), youths reported feeling extremely close to their mothers in 44 percent of cases and extremely close to their fathers in 19 percent of cases (p<.001, Wilcoxon matched pairs test).

A series of questions was also asked, of both parents and youths, about parental control over youths. There were no group differences on any of these variables.

TABLE 14   GENERAL PARENT-YOUTH RELATIONSHIP BY GROUP

Variable[a]	Category	Percentage of		p[b] Var
		Experimental Group	Control Group	
Quality of parenting[c]	**Scoring Range:**			
Parent view	21-25	23	27	—
5 items scored 5-25; $a = .640$	18-20	36	29	
	15-17	26	27	
	11-14	15	17	
Youth view	30-34	16	10	—
7 items scored 7-35; $a = .698$	25-29	35	35	
	20-24	33	31	
	10-19	16	17	
Asked of youths				
How close do you feel to your:				
father ($n = 54$)	extremely	26	36	—
	quite	44	32	
	fairly	26	23	
	not very	4	10	
mother	extremely	70	80	—
	quite	26	11	
	fairly	5	6	
	not very	0	4	
How much do you want to be like:				
father	very much	22	16	—
	somewhat	9	28	
	a little	30	25	
	not much	17	3	
	not at all	22	28	
mother	very much	23	31	—
	somewhat	26	24	
	a little	35	26	
	not much	2	4	
	not at all	14	16	
How much influence do you feel	always	14	11	—
you have in family decisions	generally	14	20	
that affect you?	sometimes	64	54	
	hardly ever	5	7	
	never	5	7	

[a] $N = 99$ for youth items, 102 for parent items, unless otherwise indicated.

[b] The two-tailed p value, based on the Mann-Whitney U test, was reported if less than .100, followed by the percent of variance accounted for by group membership.

[c] Items reflect parent-youth communication, parental fairness, and parental restraint in use of coercion; no group differences were found for single items on these scales.

Social Patterns of Youths

There were no group differences on any of the social-patterns variables. Sample statistics are reported here to provide a description of this aspect of the lives of these young people. The sample divided evenly in the importance they attach to their friends: 24 percent saw friends as very important, 26 percent as quite important, 22 percent as somewhat important, and 27 percent as not very important. Seventy-eight percent said they made friends easily. Only 5 percent did not feel free to invite friends over to their house. If youths thought they were in serious trouble, 75 percent would go to their parents for advice, 13 percent to adults outside the family, and 12 percent to their peers. Seventy-one percent of the parents reported knowing most or all of their child's friends. Only 8 percent of parents regarded their child's friends as "not the kind of people to be with."

Youths were asked whether or not they were acquainted with persons in a variety of adult roles—doctor, factory worker, policeman, cleaning person, and so on—21 roles in all. The idea was that youths with higher occupational aspirations might seek out persons with occupations of higher status; or, regardless of their intent, exposure to persons in occupations of higher status might eventually be important in the formation of occupational aspirations by youths. On the average, youths knew persons in 8.4 of these roles. There were no overall group differences. The best known roles were: teacher—known by 69 percent of the sample, factory worker—67 percent, and minister—62 percent. For purposes of further analysis, roles were ranked by their prestige, as indicated by the Hollingshead scale (1975, Note 7), with doctor, lawyer, and dentist having the highest status, cleaning person and gas station attendant the lowest status. Again, there were no group differences.

Use of Leisure Time by Youths

The most frequent leisure activities of members of the sample were sports (81 percent), cooking (79 percent), and making things (77 percent). Sports participants engaged in such activities an average 4.7 times weekly and had been playing sports for 3.5 years. Those who cooked meals did so an average 4.3 times a week and had been cooking for 3.4 years. Persons who made things, admittedly a broad category, did so an average 2.8 times a week and had been doing so for 2.7 years. Other leisure activities of these teenagers were as follows: 12 percent played a musical instrument; 38 percent collected things; 32 percent belonged to a club or church or community organization. Thirty-five percent said they attended church regularly, 31 percent sometimes, and 33 percent never. Reading for pleasure was infrequent: 47 percent engaged in reading for pleasure less than one day a week. There were gender differences for three variables: 90 percent of boys, but only 68 percent of girls participated in sports ($p = .006$); 17 percent of boys but only 5 percent of girls played a musical instrument ($p = .074$); and 88 percent of girls but only 74 percent of boys cooked meals ($p = .098$). There were no group differences on any of these variables.

Time Use by Parents

Forty-six percent of the parent respondents attended some kind of group meeting at least once a week. Just under half of the mothers (45 percent) and less than one in five fathers (18 percent) belonged to a church. Virtually none of them belonged to church organizations, clubs, social groups, neighborhood action groups, or any other kind of group. In light of these findings, frequency of meeting attendance is puzzling; perhaps these were school-related meetings. In any event, it is clear that these parents were not joiners of formal organizations.

Almost all of the parents were registered to vote (92 percent of mothers, 94 percent of fathers); most of them had voted in the last presidential election before being interviewed (77 percent of mothers, 90 percent of fathers). For most parents in the sample, the presidential election referred to was the 1972 contest between Richard Nixon and George McGovern. About half the parents voted in the last mayoral election (46 percent of mothers, 58 percent of fathers); less than half had ever attended a school board, city council, or planning commission meeting (41 percent of mothers, 27 percent of fathers).

The principal source of news for these parents was television, with 96 percent of the families having a set and 83 percent watching the national news every day. About seven out of ten (71 percent) subscribed to and read a newspaper daily. Almost half subscribed to magazines. There were no group differences on any of these variables.

Group Similarities in Teenagers and Families

While this report has focused on the effects of preschool education, it is also possible to draw a picture of how the experimental group and the control group were alike as they passed through their teenage years. This portrait emerges from data presented above and in chapter 2. Here it is drawn in broader strokes to convey a general impression.

In about half of the families, one or both of the parents were out of work, and the family received welfare assistance. Those who worked at all were very likely to have unskilled jobs. In about half of the families, the father was not present; in one out of four of these single-parent families, the mother was employed. Parents averaged a ninth-grade education. These families, with an average of over six children, were crowded into average-size residences, with more persons in residence than there were rooms.

These parents were almost all registered to vote and had voted in the 1972 presidential election. They read the newspaper and watched the news on television daily. However, they seldom joined organizations, even churches. One in two of the mothers belonged to a church, and only one in five of the fathers.

Two out of three youths in the sample had a part-time job at one time or another. The average worker made two dollars an hour, worked 14 hours a week, and had been employed almost a year. Four out of five of these young people played sports five days a week, helped with the cooking at home, and liked to make things. Half of them engaged in reading for pleasure less than once a week. They made friends easily and felt free to invite them into their homes. Three out of four youths would go to their parents if they were in trouble.

V. Summary and Causal Model

Summary

The Perry Preschool Project is a longitudinal experiment designed to reveal the effects of early educational intervention on disadvantaged young people. In this monograph, the effects of the preschool program were traced from age 3 through age 15.

The pattern of causes and effects was as follows. The children in the sample started out in a condition of poverty and appeared to have low cognitive ability. Preschool education provided the experimental group with cognitive stimulation so that their cognitive ability was higher upon school entry than it would have been otherwise. From this initial position, they began to experience and demonstrate greater success in school: greater commitment to schooling, higher school achievement, and reinforcement of a more success-oriented role by teachers, parents, and peers. Being more strongly bound to school success, they engaged in deviant behavior less frequently, first in the classroom and later in the community. Our prediction is that they will reap the rewards of greater school success: higher educational attainment, higher occupational status, and higher income.

The study was an examination of the lives of 123 children who were born with the odds against them—poor, apparently destined for school failure, and black in a country which discriminated against blacks. Each year from 1962 to 1965, children were assigned to an experimental group or a control group so as to assure group equivalence in initial cognitive ability, sex ratio, and socioeconomic status. The two resultant groups were indeed equivalent on almost all socioeconomic characteristics of families at project entry and when measured again 11 years later. Children in the experimental group attended a group preschool program 12½ hours a week and were visited at home with their mothers 1½ hours a week—one school year for the first wave of children, two school years for the remaining four waves. The goal of the program was to contribute to the intellectual development and education of each child. Between ages 3 and 15, children were assessed by a total of 48 measures—IQ tests, school achievement tests, child rating scales, parent and youth interviews, and school records. The median rate of missing data across all these measures was only 5 percent.

The effects of preschool education on school performance and experience, as described by the interpretive framework presented in chapter 1, were borne out by the data. Improvement in the cognitive ability at school entry of children who attended preschool was indicated by their increased IQs during kindergarten and first grade. Greater school achievement for these children was shown by higher achievement test scores during elementary school and substantially higher scores at eighth grade when compared to control-group children. Greater commitment to schooling was shown by a higher value placed on schooling by teenagers and by several other aspects of commitment to schooling. Reinforcement of a more positive student role for children who attended preschool was represented by more highly rated social development in elementary school, fewer years spent receiving special education services throughout their years in the public schools, and greater satisfaction and aspirations by parents with regard to the schooling of their children.

The effects of early childhood intervention on deviant behavior, as described in our interpretive framework, were also borne out by the data. Decreased deviant behavior at school by children who attended preschool was indicated by more favorably rated classroom conduct and personal behavior during elementary school and by teenagers' reports of being kept after school less often. Decreased delinquent behavior was shown by lower frequencies of self-reported delinquent behavior and serious delinquent behavior. A possible trend towards future employment success was shown by the fact that more teenagers who had attended preschool had a current job than did members of the control group. Group differences were not found in the categories of self concept, general parent-youth relationship (aside from scholastic attitudes), social patterns and use of time by youths, or use of time by parents.

Causal Model

The Perry Preschool study can no longer be regarded as a simple evaluation of a program. As data accumulate, it is clear that we are viewing a complex network of causes and effects. The preschool intervention has been successful over the years because its effects became the causes of other effects as well. In fact, the chain of causes and effects described briefly in the beginning of this chapter and more extensively in chapter 1 may be viewed as a causal model and analyzed by the procedures of path analysis. The application of these procedures to the study is described in appendix C; the results are presented in this chapter.

Figure 1 portrays a four-phase model. The three variables in phase 1 are preschool education, family socioeconomic status, and cognitive ability prior to preschool. In phase 2 the variable is cognitive ability at school entry. In phase 3 there are three variables: commitment to schooling, school achievement, and years spent receiving special education services. For phase 4 the only variable measured was delinquent behavior.

Figure 8 presents the causal model for the Perry Preschool study through age 15. For each arrow pointing from a cause to an effect, there is a statistically significant ($p<.05$) path coefficient (i.e., the beta weight). Where there is no arrow, no statistically significant path was found. Paths were investigated from one phase to the next, but paths between concurrent variables, such as commitment and achievement, were not made a part of the causal model at this time. The figure at the bottom of some of the boxes is the percentage of variance in that variable accounted for by this causal model.

Figure 8 may be described as follows. Preschool education leads to increased commitment to schooling and increased cognitive ability at school entry (the latter after the effect of cognitive ability prior to preschool has been taken into account). Family socioeconomic status, even though restricted to impoverished families and unrelated to cognitive ability within this sample, is still an antecedent of school achievement. Cognitive ability at school entry is indeed a gateway to better school performance, with a higher cognitive ability at school entry leading to greater commitment to schooling, higher school achievement and fewer years spent receiving special education services. Commitment to schooling and fewer years in special education combined in leading to fewer delinquent offenses, while achievement led to more delinquent offenses.

65

FIGURE 8   CAUSAL MODEL FOR THE PERRY PRESCHOOL STUDY, AGES 3-15

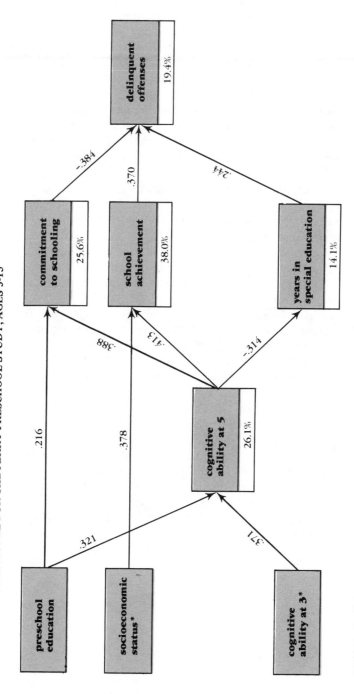

NOTES: Coefficients are beta weights, each controlling for all other variables with arrows into the variable in question. Arrows and coefficients appear only when the relationship had a statistical significance of *p* less than .05. Where variables in different phases are not connected by arrows, there was no statistically significant relationship. The percentage at the bottom of boxes is the percentage of variance in that variable accounted for by variables with arrows going into the variable in question. Thanks to Richard Zeller for his timely assistance.

*Range of the variable restricted to lower portion.

This finding of a positive relationship between achievement and delinquency corroborates a finding of G. Jensen (1976) based on re-analysis of data gathered by Wolfgang, Figlio, and Sellin (1972). He found that, while the general relationship between school achievement and delinquency was negative (as achievement went up, delinquency went down), at the lowest level of school achievement there was a reversal of the pattern. Thus, if youths were raised from the lowest percentile of school achievement to the next lowest percentile, the prediction would be that their delinquency would increase. Such a finding highlights the importance of the systematic approach taken here. The Perry Preschool intervention led not only to improved achievement, but also to increased commitment to schooling and fewer years in special education. Persons with better-than-the-worst school achievement might be more capable of delinquent behavior. But when an intervention had a broader effect on their school experience and performance, their delinquent behavior decreased.

Commitment to schooling was a variable of surprising strength in this analysis—directly affected by preschool education, closely related to school achievement (correlated at .561), and a predictor of reduced delinquency. The variable was an amalgam of elementary teacher ratings, scholastic attitudes and aspirations of teenagers, and whether or not the teenagers did homework. Though its internal consistency was quite low (an alpha coefficient of .491), it is clear that the concept of commitment has great durability. The direct relationship between commitment and preschool education suggests that the direct effects of preschool were motivational as well as cognitive. We assumed that commitment to schooling began as a response to school success. The data suggest a slight reformulation: *commitment began as a response to a cognitively stimulating preschool environment.*

The basic validation of the causal model in these findings suggests to us that the transactional approach taken in chapter 1, balancing personal motivation and performance against social reinforcement, has considerable explanatory power. In fact, our inclusion of cognitive ability at school entry as a solitary gateway for preschool effects might come to be seen as a distortion of the causal model. Although cognitive ability and preschool education have long been linked (in something of a shotgun wedding, one might say), it may be that an equally important benefit of preschool is that it provides disadvantaged children with a more favorable entry into the success flow of the school, increasing their commitment to the institution as well as their ability to meet its task-oriented demands, in short, providing a social and emotional adaptation as well as an academic or cognitive head start.

VI. Economic Implications of the Study

If early intervention programs demonstrate returns to society on investment, they will win the support of investors concerned about the society. Early intervention programs cost money and are directed at families without enough money to pay for them. If early intervention programs are to exist, they need the support of investors.

An economic analysis of the costs and benefits of the Perry Preschool program was conducted with data collected through 1973 (Weber, Foster, & Weikart, 1978). The approach was that of marginal benefit-cost analysis, that is, the differences in expense between the experimental group and the control group were used. Findings were calculated separately for one year of preschool (Wave Zero) and two years of preschool (Waves One through Four). Since the findings for two years of preschool are based on a larger sample (95 children with 48 attending preschool) than the findings for one year (28 children with 13 attending preschool), they are more reliable and will be emphasized in this summary. In order to correct for the effects of inflation (which occurred at a certain rate between 1958 and 1973, but might be more or less during some other period), the findings of the analysis were originally presented in 1958 constant dollars. Those same findings are presented here converted to 1979 constant dollars by multiplying them by 251 percent, the rate of inflation from 1958 to 1979.* This conversion did not affect the ratio of costs to benefits.

The benefits of preschool education outweighed the costs. The undiscounted benefits of two years of preschool education in 1979 dollars were $14,819 per child against a two-year program cost of $5,984 per child ($2,992 per year)—a 248 percent return on the original investment. The internal rate of return on the investment was calculated to be 3.7 percent; the internal rate of return is a discount rate which indicates the average earning power of the investment in the project. In other words, the analysis showed that investment in preschool education was equivalent to an investment receiving 3.7 percent interest over several decades. (The internal rate of return for one year of preschool was calculated to be 9.5 percent.) There are reasons to believe that this is a conservative estimate, reasons which will be noted in the following paragraphs. A major conservative factor in the analysis was noted by Grawe in his commentary on the work (Weber et al., 1978, p. 66)—that the analysis did not take into account the effects of inflation:

> If one were to project long-term inflation as unlikely to fall below, say, 5%, then the calculated rates of return would be 14.5% to one year in the project and 8.7% to two years. These values would easily bracket the range of acceptable nominal returns to long-run investments.

The cost estimate employed was the total resource cost, that is, the total public cost of the program plus the total private cost. At least 75 percent of the cost incurred was due to teacher salaries, which, in 1979 dollars, amounted to $52,670 per year for four teachers, an average annual teacher salary of $13,167. (Teachers were paid according to the local school salary schedule.) In addition to teacher salaries, the school system had the cost of supplies, building maintenance, and the Special Services Support staff (estimated to have spent 10 percent of their time on the project). Families covered the additional cost of school clothing. There were no transportation costs since the preschool was within walking distance (Weber et al., 1978, p. 33).

---

*Based on the Consumer Price Index of November 1979, seasonally adjusted (Council of Economic Advisers, 1979) and the 1958 CPI (Bureau of Labor Statistics, 1978).

70

Figure 9 shows the costs and benefits of two years of preschool education by category. In brief, these benefits were: (1) $668 per child from the mother's released time while the child attended preschool, an immediate benefit; (2) $3,353 per child saved by the public schools because children with preschool had fewer years in special education or retentions in grade; and (3) $10,798 per child in increased lifetime earnings, projected on the basis of projected educational level using data from the 1970 Census. These benefits are more fully explained below.

Mother's Released Time

While children attended preschool, their mothers' time was released for other activities besides providing care for their children. Thus the mothers could devote additional time to providing care for the remaining children in the home, to other home responsibilities, possibly to employment outside the home, or to

FIGURE 9   ECONOMIC COSTS & BENEFITS PER CHILD OF TWO YEARS OF THE PERRY PRESCHOOL PROGRAM[a]

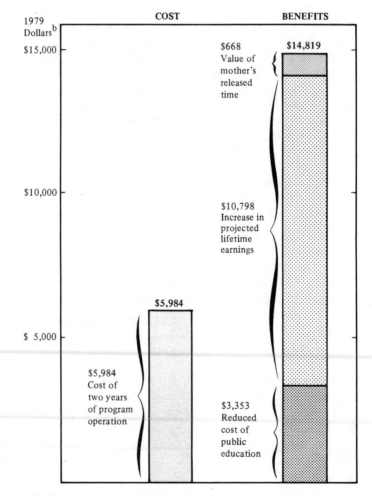

[a]Based on Weber, Foster, & Weikart, 1978, p. xi.

[b]Consumer Price Index of November, 1979, seasonally adjusted.

leisure activities. Had there been no preschool, it was assumed that, out of each 2½ hour session, the mother would have spent a total of 1 hour with the child. Over a school year, the average child attended 90 percent of the 145 preschool sessions, thereby releasing mothers for 130.5 hours a year. However, mothers' time was occupied during the 80 percent of the 30 scheduled home visits (1½ hours each) which they attended—a total of 36 hours a year. Hill and Stafford (1974) estimated the average wage rate of a homemaker at $1.41 an hour in 1958 dollars, which converts to $3.54 in 1979 dollars. The mothers' time released while the child was in preschool minus the mothers' time occupied by home visits yields a net time released of 94.5 hours a year. Multiplied by $3.54 an hour, the estimated total value of a mother's time released by the program was $334 a year.

Public School Savings

A child who attends a public school in the United States may be treated in one of three ways: (1) he or she may receive regular educational placement, proceeding through school with classmates one grade at a time; (2) he or she may be held back one or more grades, each time joining another group of classmates and proceeding with them one grade at a time; or (3) he or she may be placed in some form of special education, leaving classmates some of the time or all of the time, and being labeled as in need of special help and unable to cope with the normal demands of classroom life. Grade retention essentially doubles the cost of completing a particular grade. According to Weber et al. (1978, p. 46), self-contained special education (total removal from a regular classroom) increased the cost of schooling by 143 percent during the school year; integrated special education (removal from a classroom part of the time) increased the cost of schooling by 169 percent per school year; and institutionalized care (school district contribution only) increased costs by 187 percent per school year. For each program, costs included portions of the salaries of a variety of school personnel (i.e., teachers, principals, librarians, guidance personnel, clerical staff, and aides), salaries of special services staff for special education programs, administration, attendance and health services, plant operation and maintenance, fixed charges, capital outlay, student body charges, government aid for instruction programs, and transportation costs. The private resource costs of education were primarily foregone earnings—if an individual were not in school, he or she might have been gainfully employed. Other private resource costs were the cost of books, supplies, school clothes, and so forth.

Based on 1973 findings for educational placement, Weber et al. (1978, pp. 43-45) projected the education placements for elementary and secondary school. After correcting for a drop-out rate expected to be equal for the experimental and control groups (p. 9), overall projections for the number of student years spent in special education (of all types) came to 75.1 years for the experimental group and 167.6 for the control group. Our examination of special education records in 1979 indicated that the actual number of years spent in special education was 55.7 for the experimental group and 135.3 for the control group. The actual rate for the experimental group was 74 percent of the projected rate. The actual rate for the control group was 81 percent of the projected rate. Thus, while the projections were somewhat higher than the actual rates of special education placement, the marginal difference was actually *greater* than the projected marginal difference, by 7 percent. The increase improves the cost-benefit ratio, but by very little. The more important point is that the projected rate of differential placement in special education was actually found to be conservative in its estimate of the economic benefits of preschool education.

Calculating the savings of less expensive schooling on an annual basis, it was found that the marginal benefits for children who attended preschool over those who did not were $3,353 over the course of their schooling, on the basis of data and projections in 1973. The actual marginal benefits are known to have been greater, although the precise dollar amounts depended on actual expenditures during 1973-1980 and remain to be determined.

Increase in Projected Lifetime Earnings

Projected lifetime earnings for members of the sample were based on extrapolations from their special education status and earnings data for black males and females from the 1970 Census (*Occupational Characteristics,* 1973). The Census reports earnings for black males and females by years of school completed, but not by special education status. Therefore the following assumptions were made:

(1) If a person spent three-fourths or more of his or her school years in special education, he or she would have earnings equivalent to the median earnings of black males or females with less than eight years of education.

(2) If a person spent one-half to three-fourths of school years in special education, earnings would be equivalent to the median earnings of black males or females with eight to eleven years of education.

(3) If a person spent less than half of school years in special education, earnings would be equivalent to the median earnings of black males and females with a "low twelve years of education." It was assumed for purposes of the analysis that no one would attend college.

Projected earnings took into account the factor of economic growth during the lifetimes of the persons involved. The projected marginal increase in lifetime earnings of the experimental group over the control group was $10,798 per person in 1979 dollars. This benefit alone came close to doubling the initial preschool investment.

While the relationship between special education status and lifetime earnings should be verified by longitudinal data, there are reasons to believe that it is a conservative estimate. As mentioned above, projected years in special education were an underestimate of the marginal difference in actual years of special education found in 1979. Dropout rates were assumed to be equivalent across groups, although there is a conceptual rationale and some preliminary data (Weikart & Schweinhart, 1979, Note 8) to suggest that the dropout rate for the experimental group is lower. There is also preliminary data suggesting that some members of the sample are attending college.

Other potential benefits include the reduced rate of delinquency, which will result in savings for the victims of crimes and savings in police and court processing. There is a possibility of savings through a decreased need for welfare assistance and lower rate of usage of various social services. Finally, there is the possibility of an increase in labor-force participation, which would render even greater the marginal benefits in projected earnings. These potential benefits remain to be calculated as part of a future benefit-cost analysis.

VII. The Perry Preschool Study in Context

The purpose of this chapter is to place the findings of the Perry Preschool study in the broader context of early childhood intervention efforts of the past two decades. The findings reported in this monograph are highly favorable to the potential of early childhood intervention. They are in direct opposition to the widespread belief that early childhood interventions cannot "work," having at best a temporary effect on IQ. A close and careful examination of the grounds for the belief that preschool cannot work is in order. It is particularly important to see this question in historical perspective, since the evidence has accumulated over time and has resulted in general mood swings from optimism to pessimism and now back to a guarded optimism.

Early Intervention Research: A Brief History

Social scientists and social reformers joined together in the 1960s in an effort to deal effectively with problems of poverty through programs of early intervention. Several research projects were initiated at the local level at this time—Deutsch in New York City, Gray and Klaus in Murfreesboro, Tennessee, and Weikart in Ypsilanti, Michigan. Hunt (1961) and Bloom (1964) presented reviews of psychological research which suggested that early life experiences were crucial in the formation of intelligence and cognitive development. The concept received dramatic support from a long-term follow-up by Skeels (1966) of a small study originally reported by Skeels and Dye (1939), in which a modest program in an orphanage had led to IQ gains of almost two standard deviations. Twenty-one years later the results, though based on a small sample, were phenomenal. In the experimental group, average years of schooling were 11.7, 11 of 13 were married, and all were self-supporting. In the control group, average years of schooling were 4.0, 2 of 11 living subjects were married, 7 had marginal jobs, and 4 continued to be institutionalized. These findings surely depended on factors specific to the study and its context. Nevertheless, they indicated that an early intervention program could literally make the difference between success and failure in the lives of its participants.

Concurrent with these intellectual stirrings was the War on Poverty, a concerted effort to fight our most intensely felt social problems through social and educational programs. Project Head Start, a national program of compensatory preschool education, was born. This project and certain local preschool programs became the crucible for testing the effects of early intervention on subsequent development. The first test became whether preschool education could improve IQ and school achievement.

The first wave of findings on the cognitive benefits of preschool education was very encouraging. Several studies of local programs (e.g., Deutsch, 1971; Klaus & Gray, 1968; Weikart, 1967) found that preschool education led to increased IQs for disadvantaged children. Since IQ was meant to predict school success, it looked as if the cognitive effect of early experience was being confirmed.

This optimism was shattered by events of the next few years. The local experimental studies began to find that the initial IQ gains disappeared a year or two after the end of the preschool program. The first national evaluation of Project Head Start (Westinghouse Learning Corporation & Ohio University, 1969), despite its hastiness and methodological shortcomings, made the clear announcement that the project had almost no positive impact on cognitive performance. Zigler and Butterfield (1968) called into question even the ephemeral gains in IQ, carrying out studies which suggested that preschool-induced IQ gains represented motivational factors rather than improvement in formal cognitive processes.*

A widespread mood of pessimism about early intervention was developing. The following epitaphs appeared in the *Harvard Educational Review*:

> Intervention programs . . . fail after an initial spurt in IQ scores . . . . [Baratz & Baratz, 1970, p. 41]

> Programs of compensatory education seem to have no reliable and lasting effect. [Cronbach, 1969, p. 340]

> Compensatory education has been tried and it apparently has failed. [Jensen, 1969, p. 1]

Attempts to explain the apparent failure of early intervention came immediately. Baratz and Baratz (1970) attributed this failure to incorrect assumptions in early intervention about some general inadequacy in poor blacks. Several critics suggested that the timing of preschool intervention was wrong, Hunt (1969) arguing for earlier intervention (during infancy), Elkind (1969) arguing for later intervention (during the elementary school years).

A major critic of early intervention has been Arthur Jensen (1969). Over the years he has persistently come to the defense of IQ tests and has insisted that they show that the average black person is less intelligent than the average white person (see Jensen, 1980). Early intervention does not work, he said, because it seeks to change IQ, but IQ is largely a matter of inheritance and therefore cannot be permanently altered.

The Perry Preschool study provides evidence which is open to several interpretations concerning the extent to which cognitive ability is a predetermined, hereditary trait. By one interpretation, the disappearance of the heightened cognitive ability induced by preschool education suggests that cognitive ability is a trait which cannot be altered permanently; or the gains themselves may have represented not a true change in cognitive ability but rather a temporary distortion in the meaning and validity of the test. However, we have advanced another interpretation (in chapter 3)—that cognitive ability is always under the influence of the environment, whether a preschool or elementary school environment or any other context in which one spends a great deal of time. Since some environments, such as those associated with one's socioeconomic status, are persistent if not permanent, their effects can indeed be long-term. Much effort has been expended by Jensen and others in building a case against interventions which seek to improve cognitive ability. The alternative challenge is to design educational environments that consistently stimulate and support children's cognitive growth.

A second generation of articulate skeptics about the efficacy of early intervention is represented by deLone (1978) and Ogbu (1978), both of the Carnegie Council on Children. In the words of Ogbu (p. 98), "Compensatory education programs, both preventive and remedial, fail to produce significant improvement in the school performance of black children . . . ." But let us consider what it really means to say that an early intervention "works" or is successful.

---

*The congruity between their research and the research reported in this monograph is worth noting, i.e., a relationship between preschool-induced IQ gains and motivational processes. A crucial difference, however, is that Zigler and Butterfield dismissed the motivational differences as a byproduct of testing, whereas we found them to be more fundamental, persisting throughout schooling.

Ogbu identifies the objective of early childhood intervention programs as "enabling poor and black children to perform in elementary school at the same level as their white middle-class peers" (p. 94); this objective, he claims, promotes a "one-generation up-and-out-from-poverty" strategy (Hughes & Hughes, 1972, p. 10). We certainly agree that equalizing the educational opportunities of children regardless of their background is the basic rationale for early childhood intervention. But we do not agree that any intervention program of a few years' duration can legitimately be expected to achieve this goal by itself. Perhaps the rhetoric of justification has been less cautious than warranted by reasonable expectations. The Carnegie Council on Children is right to emphasize the immensity of the task of achieving equal opportunity in our society. As the late Ira Gordon (1979, p. 2) has said, "We continue to go through a cycle of selecting a cause and designing a single solution to problems in spite of our knowledge that life is complex and there are no simple answers." The goal of equal opportunity surely requires a time span of generations and a coordinated set of public policies that promote private initiatives as well as provide a range of timely and effective programs of intervention. A realistic objective for an early intervention program, taken in isolation from broader policies, is surely no more than to *help* narrow the existing gaps in educational opportunity through educationally significant improvements in children's performance and experience in the schools. Further, we trust that the findings reported in this monograph indicate that the earlier preoccupation with IQ as the sole criterion of early intervention effectiveness must be replaced by a broader, long-term definition of school success.

Recent evidence, not the least of which is reported in this monograph, shows that early intervention programs can in fact have important, lasting effects. DeLone (1978) hurried past these findings, relegating them to a peripheral footnote (p. 237). The following section reports the evidence in some detail.

The Maturing of Early Intervention Research

In the 1960s, thousands of early childhood programs were organized. They were an expression of the desire for service attached to the great mood of social reform that crested in the latter part of the decade. National Head Start, initiated in the summer of 1965, was simply the most visible of such programs. Less visible, but of growing importance, are the small number of scientifically designed early intervention studies that began during the sixties. These studies, which had not been widely publicized outside professional circles, have gradually accumulated information about the long-term impact of early intervention. The programs under study served a diverse, though primarily disadvantaged, population of children and their families. Most of the projects were in the eastern half of the United States. There was little contact from one project staff to another, though the principal investigators maintained a degree of professional contact. The research designs were independently evolved, with little in common as to age of participants, instrumentation, follow-up procedures, curriculum, or service delivery system. Perhaps the most common element was the widespread assessment of program outcomes by the Stanford-Binet Intelligence Scale.

It was these studies which served as the domain to be reviewed for findings on early childhood intervention (Hawkridge, Chalupsky, & Roberts, 1968;

78

Bronfenbrenner, 1974; White et al., 1973; Smilansky, 1979, Note 9). A general conclusion of these reviews was that these studies demonstrated the long-term failure of early childhood intervention. Another theme, particularly strong in the work of Bronfenbrenner (1974), was that these studies indicated that home-based, parent-focused programs were more effective than center-based, child-focused programs.

In 1975 Irving Lazar and Edith Grotberg conceived the idea of a central pooling of data from these early studies with new funding to revive lagging studies and new data collection which would ask new questions. With the support of the U. S. Administration for Children, Youth, and Families, the Consortium for Longitudinal Studies was established, with a central staff at Cornell University. Its purpose is to provide limited aid to the individual investigators for continued data collection and to carry out a secondary analysis of original and newly collected information on the impact of early intervention on children's later performance in school, on their families, and on society.

At Cornell, Irving Lazar, Richard Darlington, and their colleagues have been conducting the secondary data analysis. The presentations of Consortium findings have generally been made by Lazar and authored by his group. Each of the individual investigators, including the authors of this monograph, has been responsible for reporting the findings of his or her own study. The arrangements of the Consortium are a rarity in scientific research. The richness of the data, unavailable elsewhere, has made such a venture worth undertaking.

Consortium Methodology

Basic descriptions of the projects in the Consortium are listed in table 15. Projects had either experimental or quasi-experimental designs. The programs were either center-based or home-based, or had both components. There were programs for infants, toddlers, and children of preschool age and early elementary-school age. The programs lasted from one to five years. Except for one project sample which was 43 percent black and another which was 65 percent black, project samples were at least 89 percent black. Families in the samples had very low socioeconomic positions (as measured by the Hollingshead index), with Perry Preschool families the lowest among the group. Mothers' education levels were lowest in the Early Training Project (9.2) and the Perry Preschool Project (9.4), ranging up to 11.1 in the New Haven study. Similarly, numbers of siblings were highest in the Early Training and Perry studies (4.0), with the lowest number in the Harlem study (2.4). The Harlem study sample was all male; in other projects the proportion of females ranged from 42 to 56 percent. In terms of cognitive ability at project entry, the Perry Preschool sample was the lowest, with a mean IQ of 79; mean IQs for other samples ranged from 88 to 94.

In the most recent secondary analysis (Consortium for Longitudinal Studies, 1978; see also Consortium, 1980), projects were analyzed separately by parallel procedures. Then, overall statistical significance was determined by pooling procedures (Consortium, 1978, pp. 33-34). The secondary analysis team also contended with issues of non-equivalence of instrumentation, age differences at measurement, and sample attrition. Data analyzed included information on children's cognitive ability, achievement orientation, school achievement, special education and grade retention, and the satisfaction and scholastic aspirations of mothers for their children.

TABLE 15[a] PROJECTS IN THE CONSORTIUM FOR LONGITUDINAL STUDIES

Project	Originator(s)	Design	Delivery System Center &/or Home		Age at Entry (years)	Program Duration (years)
Perry Preschool	Weikart	Experimental	yes	yes	3-4	1-2
Parent Education	Gordon	Experimental	no	yes	0-2	1-3
Early Training	Gray	Experimental	yes	yes	4-5	1-2
Harlem Training	Palmer	Experimental	yes	no	2-3	1-2
Philadelphia	Beller	Quasi-experimental	yes	no	4	1
Mother-Child Home	Levenstein	Quasi-experimental	no	yes	2-3	1-2
Head Start Curricula	Miller	Quasi-experimental	yes	some[b]	4	1
New Haven Follow Through	Zigler	Quasi-experimental	yes	no	5	4
Institute for Developmental Studies	Deutsch & Deutsch	Quasi-experimental	yes	no	4	5
Curriculum Comparison	Karnes	Experimental[c]	yes	no	4	1-2
Micro-Social Learning	Woolman	Quasi-experimental	yes	no	4-5	1-4
Family Oriented Home Visitor	Gray	Experimental	no	yes	1-2	1-2
Curriculum Demonstration	Weikart	Experimental[c]	yes	some[b]	3	2
Infant Education	Weikart & Lambie	Experimental	no	yes	1	1½

[a]Based on Table 1, p. 13 in the 1977 Consortium Report.

[b]In the Head Start Curricula project, half of one treatment group received home visits. In the Curriculum Demonstration project, three of four waves received home visits.

[c]No control groups.

Consortium Findings

Table 16 summarizes the findings of the seven relevant projects concerning the effects of early intervention on cognitive ability. In line with our analytic framework, we have focused on the improvement in cognitive ability at school entry. It is noteworthy that, as the pretest IQ of the sample increases, the IQ advantage attributed to the program decreases. Since these are experimental/control group comparisons, this pattern is not due to regression toward the mean, since that artifact affects the groups equally. We believe that it can be explained as an effect of cognitive stimulation in the environment. The reasoning is as follows: IQ level depends in part on degree of cognitive stimulation; children with higher pretest IQs presumably came from environments that were conducive to cognitive development; children with lower pretest IQs stood to benefit relatively more from a cognitively stimulating preschool environment.

The amount of IQ advantage at school entry is greatest in the four programs which enrolled children up to the time of school entry. The contributions of the programs for younger children (0-3) peaked earlier, though they were sustained for a longer period of time than in most of the programs for older children (3-6) (see also Epstein & Weikart, 1979). To the extent that lasting improvement in cognitive ability is an end in itself, the earlier the intervention, the better. To the extent that the goal is to enhance school success, there appears to be some advantage for preschool programs just prior to kindergarten.

The most important finding of the Consortium is that *early childhood intervention decreased the numbers of students placed in special education or retained in grade*. These findings for eight projects, including the Perry Preschool Project, are shown in figure 10. Each of the four projects with experimental designs had significant reductions in special education or in the combination of special education and grade retention. Among projects of quasi-experimental design, the Mother-Child Home Program had significant reductions and the New Haven Follow Through Study had a nonsignificant trend toward reduction. No difference was found in the Philadelphia Project, a finding partly explained by the minimal availability of special education services in Philadelphia during the period covered by the study. While it appears that program children in the Head Start Curricula Project were more likely to receive special education than a control group, this may have been due to the fact that the control group for this project was initially better off than the program groups. In other words, the overall finding held true in all four experimental projects and two of the quasi-experimental projects; in two quasi-experimental projects where the finding was contradicted, the discrepancy might well be explained by flaws in design or unusual circumstances.

These data regarding placement in schools have special importance for society. As indicated in the economic analysis of the Perry Preschool Project (Weber, Foster, & Weikart, 1978), special education and retention in grade cost the schools nearly twice as much as regular education placement. Further, such placement signals lower educational attainment, which translates eventually into lower income. Figure 10 indicates that the reductions in special education placement and grade retention in four of the projects were comparable in magnitude to those in the Perry Preschool Project. It is reasonable to assume that the economic implications of the Perry Preschool Project may be generalized to these other projects.

TABLE 16   IMPROVEMENT IN COGNITIVE ABILITY IN SEVEN EARLY INTERVENTION PROJECTS[a]

Project	Pretest IQ of Sample	IQ Advantage at School Entry[b]	Years' Duration of IQ Advantage
For Older Children (3-6)			
Perry Preschool	79	11	2
Early training	88	9	0
Philadelphia	91	7	4
Head Start Curricula	93	7	0
For Younger Children (0-3)			
Parent Education	91[c]	5[d]	4
Harlem Training	92	5[e]	3
Mother-Child Home	94	4	6[f]

[a] Based on Table 5 in the 1977 Consortium Report, p. 54.

[b] The IQ advantage of the program group over the control group at school entry was statistically significant at $p<.02$ in six of the seven programs, using either analysis of variance or analysis of covariance (including pretest IQ as a covariate) designs.

[c] Control group at age 3; no pretest given.

[d] The maximum IQ gain was 8 points at age 3.

[e] The maximum IQ gain was 9 points at age 4.

[f] Differences were not consistently significant during this period, probably due to the attrition in a small control group.

The Consortium found (by the technique of pooled statistical significance across projects) that early childhood intervention led to improvement in mathematics achievement from grades 3 to 5 and reading achievement at grade 3 ($p<.05$). Among specific projects, only the Mother-Child Home Program found statistically significant differences with any consistency. Though the Perry Preschool study was one of the projects analyzed, school achievement at eighth grade was not analyzed because it had not been assessed in any other project at that time. For the same reason, overall school achievement was not analyzed in the earlier grades. This exclusive focus on common instrumentation across projects has the unfortunate effect of concealing the unique strengths of individual projects.

The finding of the Perry Preschool study that parents were better satisfied with the school performance of their children was replicated in the Parent Education Program, the Mother-Child Home Program, and the Philadelphia Project. By the significance pooling technique, some corroboration was also found for the Perry finding that parents and children had higher educational aspirations for the children.

The Consortium also tested a kind of causal model which resembles some aspects of the causal model of the Perry Preschool study presented here. The Consortium's causal model found cognitive ability at school entry to be an effect of early childhood intervention and a matrix of socioeconomic variables (e.g., mother's education level, father's presence, number of siblings in the family). Cognitive ability at school entry was found to be associated with assignment to special education. The Consortium model did not include investigation of school achievement, commitment to schooling, deviant behavior, or aspects of adult success.

82

FIGURE 10   STUDENTS PLACED IN SPECIAL EDUCATION OR HELD BACK A GRADE IN EIGHT
EARLY INTERVENTION PROJECTS[a]

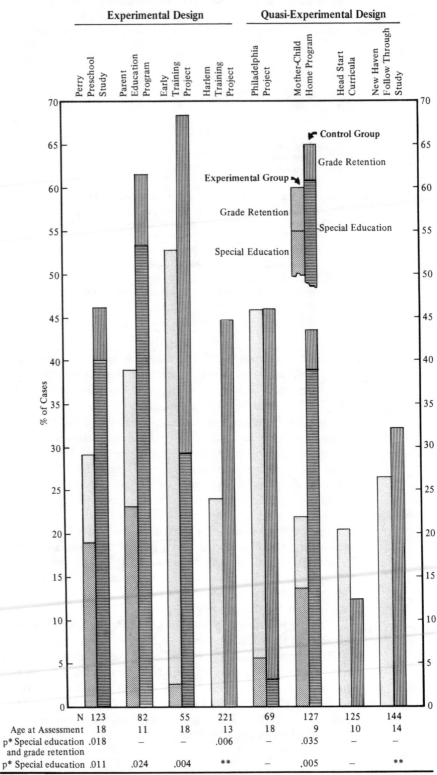

	N	Age at Assessment	p* Special education and grade retention	p* Special education
Perry Preschool Study	123	18	.018	.011
Parent Education Program	82	11	–	.024
Early Training Project	55	18	–	.004
Harlem Training Project	221	13	.006	**
Philadelphia Project	69	18	–	–
Mother-Child Home Program	127	9	.035	.005
Head Start Curricula	125	10	–	–
New Haven Follow Through Study	144	14	–	**

[a]Based on Tables 9 and 11 in the 1978 Consortium Report, pp. 69 and 71.
*p reported if less than .10.
**Special education not distinguished in these projects.

The National Effort and the Perry Project: Some Comparisons

The question of the efficacy of early intervention programs is not merely of academic interest; it has direct implications for how the United States government invests financial resources. In the 1979 fiscal year, the federal government alone spent 1.6 billion dollars in programs which brought early childhood intervention to 1.8 million children aged 0 to 5. State and local governments spent at least an additional 20 percent of this amount ($316 million) in matching funds for most of these programs. These programs and expenditures are listed in table 17. It should be noted that, while 1.6 billion dollars is a large amount of money, it was less than .3 percent of the total 1979 federal budget.

The applicability of the previously described early intervention research to the programs listed in table 17 depends on the extent to which these programs are comparable to the researched programs. To the extent that the current federal programs resemble the researched programs in purpose, population served, and program characteristics, it may be inferred that they also produce similar effects. Of course, such an inference constitutes less direct evidence than actual evaluations of the large-scale programs would provide. But given the expense, difficulty, and inevitable criticisms of large-scale evaluations, inferences from smaller studies with experimental designs may in practice be the best guides for decision-making.

Comparison of Goals

The goals of the Perry Preschool program and the other researched programs were to help disadvantaged children acquire the intellectual and social strengths they would need in school and to enable parents to better support these strengths in their children. These goals are a part of all the programs listed in table 17. They are perhaps most central to the mission of Head Start, although this program also has goals in health, mental health, and social services (see Zigler & Valentine, 1979).

The principal goal of Title XX day care is to support lower-income families in providing care for their children. (Another government policy, tax credit for child-care expenses, has this same purpose of supporting families, regardless of income.) Since Title XX day care provides an environment for young children at public expense, the societal goal of promoting equal educational opportunity comes into play. A second goal of Title XX day care has therefore been the same as that of early childhood intervention—to help disadvantaged children acquire the intellectual and social strengths they will need in school.

Comparison of Populations Served

The Perry Preschool program served disadvantaged children who were diagnosed as educable mentally retarded. The other Consortium programs also served disadvantaged children. Head Start, Title I, and Title XX day care programs are clearly targeted for disadvantaged children. A large proportion of the handicapped children served by preschool programs are classified as educable mentally retarded, learning disabled, and emotionally impaired, classifications which do not require evidence of organic handicap. In this way they are comparable to the children served in the Perry Preschool program.

TABLE 17   FEDERAL SPENDING FOR EARLY INTERVENTION PROGRAMS[a]

Program	FY79 Budget for Children 0-5	Children 0-5 Served	Per Child Federal Expenditure
Title XX Day Care[b] (Social Security Act)	$731,000,000	800,000	$914[c]
Head Start[d]	$625,000,000	369,370[e]	$1692
Title I Preschool (Elementary and Secondary Education Act)	$135,000,000[f]	378,000	$357
Handicapped Preschool Incentive and State Formula Grants	$65,000,000	217,561	$299
Appalachian Regional Commission Comprehensive Child Development	$14,000,000[g]	15,000	$933
Migrant Early Childhood	$10,000,000	101,440	$99
Total	$1,580,000,000	1,881,371[h]	$840

[a] Sources: Fauntleroy (1979) and Interagency Committee for the International Year of the Child (1979) and personal communications with responsible officials.

[b] 25 percent state and local matching.

[c] This figure is based on dividing total expenditures by the number served. The federal reimbursement rate averages $9 to $12 a day in most states. Based on a 250-day year, the per-child federal expenditure would be $2250 to $3000.

[d] 20 percent state and local matching; 10 percent from other federal sources.

[e] Full-year only.

[f] Estimate based on the fact that 7 percent of Title I children served were 3-5 years old.

[g] FY77; matched by $6,000,000 from state and local sources (43%).

[h] This total may be overestimated, since there is no straightforward way to determine the number of children receiving federal funds from more than one source.

A more detailed comparison of the Perry Preschool children (in 1962-65) and Head Start children (in 1977)* reveals that Perry Preschool children were even worse off than most Head Start children. (It was noted in the previous section that Perry Preschool children were also worse off than the children in most of the other Consortium studies.) Fewer than half as many Perry mothers completed high school (21 percent vs. 54 percent). Almost twice as many Perry families were single-parent families (47 percent vs. 27 percent). While income data were not collected from Perry families, some idea of their income (expressed in 1977 dollars) can be obtained from the Head Start data. Head Start families with no employed parent had an income of $3,944 (including welfare assistance), while Head Start families with at least one employed parent had an income of $7,337. Further analysis of the Head Start income data suggests that the average income of Perry Preschool families, in 1977 dollars, would have been $4,515. The average income of Head Start families in 1977 was $6,354. It is likely that these income differences reflect a general improvement in the quality of life throughout the society between 1962 and 1977. But the *relative* poverty of Head Start families with respect to the rest of society may be just as great as was the relative poverty of Perry Preschool families.

These comparisons suggest that current government-sponsored early intervention programs serve children who are in many cases faced with the same disadvantages as those faced by children in the Perry Preschool Project.

*Head Start figures are based on the national sample of Head Start families in the Head Start Transition study (Royster & Larson, 1978).

Comparison of Program Characteristics

The programs examined by the Consortium for Longitudinal Studies varied widely along many dimensions. The 1978 Consortium report (pp. 122-157) studied ten distinct program dimensions: age of child at entry, overall duration of program, annual duration of program, degree of parental influence, whether or not there was a center-based component, professional versus paraprofessional staff, amount of preservice training for staff, language goals for children, amount of teaching structure, and hours per year of program. By conservative procedures of data analysis, it was determined that no specific program characteristic distinguished successful programs from less successful ones.

In the High/Scope Foundation's Preschool Curriculum Demonstration Project (Weikart, Epstein, Schweinhart, & Bond, 1978), basic program characteristics were held constant, except for type of curriculum model. Three philosophically disparate curriculum models were compared: the Cognitively Oriented Curriculum (which grew out of the Perry Preschool Project); a behaviorist, programmed-learning curriculum (Bereiter & Engelmann, 1966); and a unit-based, traditional nursery-school curriculum. Each of the three programs, under conditions ensuring a high quality of implementation, was highly successful—each produced a lasting IQ gain of at least 11 points five years after preschool.

The search for discrete program characteristics which are responsible for success continues. Our own speculation has focused on the fact that projects known to be successful have a high degree of *quality control*—they are closely monitored by directors with high personal investment in the projects, with emphasis on delivery of services as scheduled, training of staff, and a general attitude of experimentation. The essential ingredients are a competent and committed staff whose director is a leader as well as an administrator. (These qualities also lead to success in elementary school programs, as attested to by the research of Edmonds, 1979.) Government regulations have only an indirect relationship to such qualities.

The Consortium programs were not intended to be representative of any particular government program, although the later Head Start programs do resemble Consortium programs in many respects. Their relationship to other programs might best be viewed as *exemplary* rather than representative, as model programs to inspire others. In this respect, a sports analogy is helpful. Roger Bannister ran the mile in 1952 in less than four minutes. His accomplishment was not negated by the facts that no other athlete had ever done it before or that many believed it to be impossible. Today, of course, with proper diet, coaching, improved techniques—and the knowledge that it can be done—all world-class athletes run the mile in less than four minutes.

Neither is the cost of operating programs like the Perry Preschool program a prohibitive factor. It will be recalled that the per-child cost of operation of the Perry Preschool program, in 1979 dollars, was $2,992 per year. The estimated cost per child of operating a Head Start program in 1979 was $2,464—including Head Start costs, local costs, and costs covered by other federal programs such as CETA and food supplement programs.* It appears that a program like the Perry Preschool could be operated at a rate of expenditure only 21 percent higher than current Head Start expenditures. Of course the categories of expenditure differ considerably. On the one hand, the Perry Preschool program employed teachers, but it did not employ nurses or social workers. On the other hand,

* Estimate provided by Douglas Klafehn of the staff of the U.S. Administration for Children, Youth, and Families.

teachers in the Perry Preschool program were paid according to the public school salary schedule, while current pay for most Head Start teachers is far lower than current public school salary schedules.

If the Perry Preschool program and other Consortium programs are indeed exemplary rather than representative, then perhaps the government can promote high-quality early childhood programs more broadly by increasing the visibility of the exemplary programs. Such strategies are already being employed in the Early Childhood Assistance Program of the U. S. Bureau of Education for the Handicapped, in which 20 million dollars a year is spent on program demonstration and outreach efforts. This is also the strategy of the National Diffusion Network of the Office (now Department) of Education, funded at a level of 10 million dollars in 1979, to promote the dissemination of programs approved by the Joint Dissemination and Review Panel. Perhaps similar strategies could be adopted within the Head Start and Title XX day care programs. Further, these strategies could focus not only on classroom practices, but also on broader methods of program operation and leadership by program directors.

Epilogue

School failure by children who live in poverty is an intractable problem. When children begin school with socioeconomic disadvantages, they too often become locked into a pattern of scholastic disadvantages. Worse yet, as they become adults, these scholastic disadvantages become their own socioeconomic disadvantages.

Where are the points of penetration which allow the cycle to be modified? To the extent that parents and teachers make snap judgments about the potential of children, they must become more patient and sensitive. To the extent that our schools place children in tracks of failure from which there is virtually no escape, they must be changed. But clearly, exhortations are not enough; and the strategies to effect such changes are long in coming.

It has been shown here that preschool education can be a part of the solution, but it is only a part. What is needed is broad planning in public policies so that government interventions are timely and effective and private initiatives are also promoted. Though some of our conclusions differ from theirs, we believe that the Carnegie Council on Children has maintained the necessary scope and level of discussion. We envision a dynamic model of society in which the role of the government is to assist individuals in their own efforts to improve the conditions of their lives. Individuals take responsibility for what they achieve; the government takes responsibility for a coordinated set of programs and policies which help persons to become autonomous and productive. Thus, individuals and government share the responsibility to lessen the effects of poverty and discrimination on children.

A basic theme in this monograph has been the relationship between commitment and achievement. First there was the commitment of the staff of the Perry Preschool Project, striving to offer the best possible program to each child enrolled. Then came children's commitment to achievement in school and a similar commitment communicated to them by teachers, parents, and peers. Commitment has both an internal, motivational aspect and an external aspect which is communicated to others. For children to continue to achieve in school, they must believe in themselves as capable students, and they must see others believing in them as well. But these beliefs cannot be based on inflated fantasies; they must be based on real achievement—the successful accomplishment of the tasks of the school.

Achievement in the society likewise requires commitment from individuals and the demonstrated commitment of institutional leaders. If such is the case, the current disenchantment with our institutions—family, schools, the government, and so on—indicates an unfortunate climate for personal and social achievement. But if we can learn to invest ourselves more fully in our institutions, and if our institutions can learn ways to reward individual responsibility and effort, perhaps we can achieve the greatness of which our society is capable.

Appendices

Appendix A:
Data Analysis
and Presentation

Our intent in writing this report was to make it accessible to the widest possible audience; that is, to analyze and present results as simply and clearly as possible, consistent with prevailing standards of statistical methodology. In keeping with this intent, it was decided to allow the experimental design of the study to stand on its own and to present simple tests of group differences in the text, while presenting the results of more complex designs for data analysis in an appendix. It was also decided that, while interval variables would be analyzed by parametric tests, the text would report analyses of nominal and ordinal variables by nonparametric tests.

In some instances, a series of variables of similar nature were summed into a scale. For each scale constructed from the age 14 school achievement test and the age 15 youth and parent interviews, the alpha coefficient of internal consistency was calculated and reported. Further, where variables were collected repeatedly over time, as with teacher ratings or achievement tests, an alpha coefficient over time was calculated and reported. The alpha coefficient is a measure of how well the items on a scale (or repeated measures) are measuring the same thing for the respondents in question (see Cronbach, Gleser, Nanda, & Rajaratnam, 1970). Technically, the alpha coefficient is obtained by subtracting the sum of item variances from the total scale variance, dividing by the scale variance, then (to correct for scale length) multiplying the result by the number of items divided by one less than the number of items.

Nominal and ordinal data in this report came from the youth interview, both parent interviews, and the teacher rating instruments. The nominal variables, each consisting of categories with no quantitative relationship to each other, were, for this report, all dichotomous variables (for example, yes/no or male/female). The rest of the variables from the indicated sources were ordinal; that is, they were made up of categories which ranked individuals in some way, but did not indicate the distance between individuals on the variable in terms of some criterion.

For each category of nominal and ordinal variables, the report presents the percentage of the experimental group and the percentage of the control group who responded to that category. Percentages are reported to the nearest whole number, so as not to introduce an unjustified precision; for this reason, total percentages may vary slightly from 100 percent. Nominal variables were analyzed by the chi-square test of the independence of groups on a particular variable. Ordinal variables were analyzed by the Mann-Whitney U test or the median test (for skewed distributions); both test the hypothesis that the distribution of the variable was the same in each group.

Interval variables in this report came from IQ and school achievement tests and from the number of years in special education. An interval variable consists of categories which rank individuals and specify the distances between them on the variable by an external criterion. Group means are reported for these variables, and they are analyzed by analysis of variance.

For each test of statistical significance, the exact, two-tailed p value was reported if it was less than .10. The p value is the probability, expressed as a proportion of 1.00, that (in this case) the group difference on a variable occurred by chance.

While the p value is commonly accepted as a means for determining statistical significance, different approaches might have been taken. Since the hypothesized direction of a group difference on an outcome variable was usually specified in advance, it would also have been legitimate to employ one-tailed rather than two-tailed tests of statistical significance; in fact the reader can easily make this conversion by dividing the reported p value by 2. On the other hand, since a bivariate approach was employed (that is, group membership and some comparison variable), it might be argued that the reported relationships are apparent rather than real, that they duplicate each other and mask other effects. The causal analysis reported in chapter 5 is an attempt to overcome this problem, as are the analyses of covariance reported in appendix B. But it should be pointed out that the approach taken is justified by the experimental design which divided the sample on the basis of group membership.

When the p value was reported, the percentage of variance accounted for by group membership was also reported. The percentage of variance estimates the magnitude or strength of association between two variables, in this case, between receiving or not receiving preschool education and the outcome variable. The square root of the proportion corresponding to this percentage is the product-moment correlation between the two variables. In analysis of variance terms, the percentage of variance is the between-groups variance divided by the total variance in the outcome variable.*

These data were stored and analyzed by programs in the University of Michigan computer system, which currently has an Amdahl 170/V7 as its central computer. Data analysis was conducted with program commands in the Michigan Interactive Data Analysis System (commands: twoway, twosample, anova, regression, and mcorr) and in the University installation of the Statistical Package for the Social Sciences (anova command used for factorial designs).

Appendix B:
Supplementary Analyses

The statistical analyses presented in the text were simple analyses of differences between the experimental group and the control group. These analyses were both parametric (analysis of variance F tests) and nonparametric (Mann-Whitney U tests for ordinal variables, median tests for ordinal variables with highly skewed distributions, and chi-square tests for nominal, dichotomous variables).

This approach was taken for three reasons. First, it capitalized on the relatively strong experimental design of the study. Second, statistical manipulation of the data actually obtained was not necessary. Third, nonparametric tests for simple group comparisons are readily available, while such tests are not readily available

---

*For nominal and ordinal data, the percent of variance was calculated to be the result of the formula: $z^2/n\text{-}1$, where z was the z score associated with the exact p value and n was the number of cases for the test (see Carr, Marascuilo, & Serlin, 1979, Note 10, for further explanation of this procedure).

for more complex factorial designs. Some argue that parametric tests are usually adequate for the analysis of nonparametric variables, but there is no guarantee that they are. In fact, since both parametric and nonparametric tests were run for our outcome variables, that proposition was put to the test here; results are reported below.

In previous monographs reporting this study, other approaches to data analysis were taken. In the first monograph (Weikart, Deloria, Lawser, & Wiegerink, 1970), outcomes were analyzed by a three-way analysis of variance which used the factors of group membership (experimental vs. control), gender, and wave. In the second monograph (Weikart, Bond, & McNeil, 1978), this analysis was again employed and presented in tandem with a separate analysis of covariance, which employed ten variables representing family and child entry characteristics.

In this monograph, in addition to the parametric and nonparametric group comparisons reported in the text, four supplemental analytic designs were employed, all of them parametric. In all of them, the principal hypothesis tested was that there was a statistically significant difference between the performance of the experimental group and the control group. These four designs were:

(1) *One-way analysis of variance*—this approach determined whether variables found to have a statistically significant group difference by nonparametric means would continue to do so by parametric means without adding other conditions.

(2) *Two-way analysis of variance*, group by wave—this approach determined whether group differences remained statistically significant, after averaging across waves.

(3) *One-way analysis of covariance*—testing group effect over and above the effects of gender, cognitive ability at age three, family socioeconomic status, mother's educational attainment, and mother's employment status.

(4) *Two-way analysis of covariance*—group by wave, over and above the effects of the above covariates: gender, cognitive ability at age three, family socioeconomic status, mother's educational attainment, and mother's employment status.

The outcome variables found to be statistically significant across groups by the procedures reported in the text were submitted to these procedures. The statistically significant group differences disappeared for only a few of these variables, as reported in the following paragraphs.

Since these analyses were seen as supplemental, they were carried out only with those variables for which group differences were reported in the text. These group differences are re-presented here in essentially the same order as they appeared in the text, with each variable signified by a short caption.

The group difference in percentage of single-parent mothers employed outside the home, reported at $p=.002$, did not differ from this value by more than .001 in any of the other procedures employed. Table A-1 presents the p values obtained for IQ and achievement test scores by the reported analysis of variance technique and by the three other supplemental techniques. The statistically significant differences for IQ at ages 4, 5, 6, and 7 were affected by no more than .02 across all the techniques. Group differences on achievement test scores, in general, were slightly less statistically significant when analysis of covariance techniques were employed. At age 7, the statistical significance of total achievement, reading, and arithmetic group differences decreased, going from a p value of less than .1 to a p value of about .1. The same was true to a lesser degree for the same scores on the age 14 achievement test, and especially for the subtest

TABLE A-1 P VALUES RESULTING FROM FOUR ANALYTIC PROCEDURES: COGNITIVE ABILITY AND SCHOOL ACHIEVEMENT

Group Difference	Analysis of Variance (reported in text)	Two-way Analysis of Variance	Analysis of Covariance	Two-way Analysis of Covariance
Stanford-Binet IQ				
Age 4	<.001	<.001	<.001	<.001
Age 5	<.001	<.001	<.001	<.001
Age 6	.017	.018	.024	.024
Age 7	.022	.022	.044	.040
Achievement Scores				
Overall	.059	.047	.093	.074
Total				
Age 7	.085	.064	.252	.216
Age 8	.082	.075	.084	.079
Age 9	.054	.044	.054	.042
Age 10	.106	.104	.037	.040
Age 14	<.001	.001	.005	.003
Reading				
Age 7	.109	.095	.240	.220
Age 9	.086	.087	.097	.095
Age 10	.078	.075	.018	.019
Age 14	.013	.023	.067	.037
Arithmetic				
Age 7	.098	.057	.238	.153
Age 8	.052	.059	.068	.073
Age 9	.074	.059	.068	.050
Age 14	.015	.004	.078	.030
Language				
Age 9	.040	.030	.035	.028
Age 10	.076	.073	.037	.038
Age 14	<.001	<.001	<.001	<.001
Age 14 Subtests				
Vocabulary	.001	.004	.010	.009
Math Computation	.075	.023	.227	.122
Math Concepts & Problems	.008	.003	.054	.022
Capitalization & Punctuation	<.001	<.001	.002	.001
Language Usage & Structure	.006	.007	.015	.007
Spelling	.004	.006	.010	.010

of mathematics computation. On the other hand, the group differences of the age 10 total achievement, reading, arithmetic, and language scores were all made more highly statistically significant by the analysis of covariance techniques. In effect, the analysis of covariance techniques smooth out the year-to-year discrepancies in the size of group differences in achievement test scores. The basic pattern of a persistent effect of preschool education on achievement test scores remains unaffected by the choice among the statistical techniques reported here.

Table A-2 presents the p values obtained for school experience and delinquency variables by the nonparametric technique reported (either U test, median test, or chi-square test) and by the supplementary techniques. School experience variables were largely unaffected by choice of technique. Group differences in elementary school motivation and thoughts about college were made slightly less statistically significant by the analysis of covariance procedures.

TABLE A-2 P VALUES RESULTING FROM FIVE ANALYTIC PROCEDURES:
SCHOOL EXPERIENCE AND DELINQUENCY

Group Difference	Nonpara-metric Test (reported in text)[a]	Analysis of Variance or X^2	Two-way Analysis of Variance	Analysis of Covariance	Two-way Analysis of Covariance
Commitment to Schooling	—	<.001	<.001	.003	.001
Elementary School Motivation	.087	.075	.081	.137	.144
Value Placed on School	.024	.052	.028	.065	.052
Importance of High School	.066	.027	.026	.043	.036
Thought About College	.077	.077	.046	.124	.092
Thought About School	.003	.016	.018	.052	.053
Do Homework	—	.006	<.001	.018	.001
Days of Homework	—	.044	.142	.075	.031
Self-rated School Ability	.009	.019	.030	.006	.005
Years in Special Education	—	.029	.031	.009	.009
Social Development	.057	.050	.052	.061	.060
Parent School Attitudes					
Satisfaction with Youth	—	.014	.010	.020	.019
Aspirations for Youth	.027	.026	.032	.019	.019
Conferences Invited by Teacher	.030	.018	.021	.002	.003
Parent-Teacher Contact Reported by Youth	—	.005	.008	.009	.006
School Conduct					
Classroom Conduct	.061	.053	.053	.107	.114
Personal Behavior	.060	.079	.083	.146	.147
Kept After School	.078	.067	.091	.041	.046
Delinquency					
Total Delinquency	.022	.189	.638	.147	.365
Serious Delinquency	.048	.227	.112	.273	.440
Take by Force	.034	.037	.057	.176	.193
Damage Institutional Property	.033	.028	.039	.079	.102
Lie About Age or ID	.079	.033	.016	.041	.037

[a]A dash indicates that an ordinal test was not used; in these instances the p value appearing in the second column was the one reported in the text.

The statistical significance of group differences in total and serious delinquency was essentially negated by parametric techniques. However, these variables were not normally distributed, with median values of 2 and maximum values of 35. In addition to these variables, several other deviancy variables also showed diminished group differences by the analysis of covariance techniques. Parametric procedures assume that the variables employed are normally distributed; they are therefore inappropriate for use with delinquency as an outcome variable. This inappropriateness is attested to by the fact that several major studies of delinquency (Empey, Lubeck, & LaPorte, 1971; Wolfgang, Figlio, & Sellin, 1972) did not employ parametric techniques to study delinquency as an outcome variable.

In summary, the experimental design of the Perry Preschool Project appears to have accomplished the purpose it was supposed to accomplish. Group differences found by simple group comparison techniques were essentially unaffected by more complex statistical techniques.

Appendix C:
Developing a Causal Model
for the Study

The framework for this report was analyzed in a consolidated way by the methodology of path or causal analysis (e.g., Blalock, 1961; Heise, 1975). This approach employs multiple regression techniques to take into account the direct contribution of each variable over and above the contributions of other variables. It takes advantage of the longitudinal nature of the study to make inferences about the hypothesized causal network. A key principle of causality is that a cause cannot occur after an effect (Heise, 1975), and a longitudinal study permits specification of the temporal order of hypothesized causes and effects. Another principle of causality is that cause and effect must make contact with each other, either directly or through mediating variables ("operators" in Heise's terminology). For example, it has been said that a long-range goal of the Perry Preschool program was to reduce juvenile delinquency. But preschool education does not make direct contact with delinquent behavior, so mediating variables are necessary. In this study we have viewed school experience and performance variables as mediating between preschool and delinquency.

The temporal order and continuity of the Perry Preschool Project made it an obvious candidate for causal analysis. Our causal analysis began with the concepts appearing in figure 1. This interpretive framework begins with three variables viewed as causes: preschool education, family socioeconomic status, and cognitive ability prior to preschool. Next comes cognitive ability at school entry, viewed as a gateway variable between preschool and background variables on the one hand and school experience and performance variables on the other. In the next phase, the variables are commitment to schooling, school achievement, and student role reinforcement. Delinquent behavior is the last specified effect which had been measured prior to this monograph. Other variables in this last phase, educational attainment and occupational status and productivity, will be included in future reports.

The next procedure was to specify each of these eight concepts as operational variables. For four of them—cognitive ability before preschool and at school entry, preschool education, and deviant behavior—the operationalization was straightforward. Cognitive ability prior to preschool (age 3) and at school entry (age 5), was determined by the IQ tests given at those times. Family socioeconomic status was the variable originally used for sample selection and group assignments, consisting of a composite of parents' educational attainment, employment status, and household density. Preschool education was a dichotomous variable based on whether a subject was in the experimental group or the control group. The index of deviant behavior employed was the self-report scale of total delinquent behavior.

The school performance and experience terms required relatively more inference and model-fitting than these other variables. School achievement had been measured six times from first grade to eighth grade. Raw scores on each test were standardized within the sample for that testing. Then, whenever a child had scores on at least five of the six tests, these scores were averaged together into a composite measure of school achievement to be used in the model.

To construct a measure of commitment to schooling, we first looked at the correlation matrix of six likely variables: elementary school motivation, value placed on schooling by teenagers, whether or not teenagers reported doing homework, their self-rated school ability, whether or not they had thought about college, and their willingness to talk to parents about what was going on at school. Four of these variables were more highly correlated with each other: elementary school motivation, value placed on schooling, homework, and thoughts about college. These four variables were standardized within the sample, then averaged together for each child who had scores on at least three of the four variables. This composite variable (whose alpha coefficient was .491) was then used as an index of commitment to schooling.

We eventually decided to use years in special education as our only index of student role reinforcement. While parent aspirations and satisfaction with the youth's school performance seemed reasonable to add to the model, they did not have statistically significant relationships with the other terms of the model, and their exclusion seemed to clarify the model.

We recognize that our operationalization of this model is only one of a variety of possibilities. Though we divided the study into four phases, we did not take full advantage of its longitudinal nature. Elementary school experience and performance is not the same as middle school experience and performance, and in fact knowledge about the relationship between the two periods is crucial to an understanding of the genesis of school success or failure. However, these questions are reserved for future study. The purpose of the present causal model is simply to demonstrate the explanatory potential of the causal-analysis approach in this longitudinal study.

The bivariate correlation matrix for the eight variables is shown in table A-3. This matrix provided preliminary information for the multiple regression analyses which followed. It was decided to look for causal paths only from one phase to the next, rather than within phases, since variables within phases were concurrent and had no clear causal priority over each other. This decision had no effect on the phase-one variables of preschool education, socioeconomic status, and cognitive ability at age 3, since the variables were minimally correlated with each other. Among phase-three variables, commitment and achievement were highly correlated with each other, but not with special education. Arguments could be made that commitment causes achievement or that achievement causes commitment. Indeed we hope to disentangle this question in future analyses. But, in the current analysis, it seemed best to leave the question unresolved.

Multiple regression analyses were carried out, using these eight variables as outcomes and predictors. In the first analysis, delinquency was predicted from commitment, achievement, and special education; all three variables were statistically significant predictors ($p<.05$). In the next three analyses, commitment, achievement, and special education were in turn treated as outcomes predicted by cognitive ability at age 5, preschool education, socioeconomic status, and cognitive ability at age 3. In each of these analyses, some predictors were statistically significant and some were not, and three more analyses were run, one for each outcome, employing only the significant predictors: commitment predicted by cognitive ability at age 5 and preschool education, achievement predicted by cognitive ability at age 5 and socioeconomic status, and special education predicted by cognitive ability at age 5 alone. In the next analysis, cognitive ability at age 5 was predicted by preschool

TABLE A-3 CAUSAL MODEL VARIABLES: BIVARIATE CORRELATION MATRIX

Variable	preschool education	socioeconomic status	cognitive ability at 3	cognitive ability at 5	commitment to schooling	school achievement	years in special education	delinquent behavior
preschool education	1.000							
socioeconomic status	.107	1.000						
cognitive ability at 3	.085	.075	1.000					
cognitive ability at 5	.353*	.212	.398*	1.000				
commitment to schooling	.353*	.123	.256*	.464*	1.000			
school achievement	.164	.466*	.312*	.493*	.561*	1.000		
years in special education	-.256*	-.064	.007	-.314*	-.320*	-.278*	1.000	
delinquent behavior	-.049	.154	.156	-.015	-.254*	.087	.264*	1.000

Note: N for these correlations was 76.

*$p<.05$

education, socioeconomic status, and cognitive ability at 3. Socioeconomic status was not a significant predictor, so another analysis employed preschool education and cognitive ability at age 3 to predict cognitive ability at age 5.

The beta weights for each pair of related variables resulting from the last analysis carried out for each outcome variable became the path coefficients reported in figure 8. A beta weight is the amount of change in a standardized outcome variable which results from one unit of change in a standardized predictor variable, all other things being equal. Also in figure 8, the percentage of variance accounted for (i.e., the squared multiple correlation) for each multiple regression analysis is specified below the outcome variable. This was used as an alternative to specifying disturbance factors for each variable. The direction from cause to effect for each path was determined by the four-phase temporal order of the model. For example, preschool education occurs before commitment to schooling and before cognitive ability at age 5, and therefore the significant beta weights are taken to indicate that preschool education causes increases in commitment to schooling and in cognitive ability at age 5.

Reference Notes

1. Sameroff, A. J. *Theoretical and empirical issues in the operationalization of transactional research.* Paper presented at the biennial meeting of the Society for Research in Child Development, San Francisco, March, 1979.

2. Werner, E. *Applications to the longitudinal study of the high-risk child on the island of Kauai.* Paper presented at the biennial meeting of the Society for Research in Child Development, San Francisco, March, 1979.

3. Sigman, M., & Parmelee, A. H. *Evidence for the transactional model in a longitudinal study of pre-term infants.* Paper presented at the biennial meeting of the Society for Research in Child Development, San Francisco, March, 1979.

4. White, K. R. *The relationship between socioeconomic status and academic achievement.* Unpublished doctoral dissertation, University of Colorado, 1976.

5. Wolf, R. M. *The identification and measurement of environmental process variables related to intelligence.* Unpublished doctoral dissertation, University of Chicago, 1964.

6. Berger, R. J., Crowley, J. E., Gold, M., & Gray, J. *Experiment in a juvenile court.* Ann Arbor: University of Michigan Institute for Social Research, 1975.

7. Hollingshead, A. B. *Working paper, Four factor index of social status.* Unpublished manuscript, 1975. (Available from author at Department of Sociology, Yale University, Box 1965, Yale Station, Conn. 06520).

8. Weikart, D. P., & Schweinhart, L. J. *Preliminary findings on the social and economic adjustment of young adults who completed an experimental preschool.* Paper presented at the annual meeting of the American Educational Research Association, San Francisco, April, 1979.

9. Smilansky, M. Priorities in education: Preschool—evidence and conclusions. *World Bank Staff Working Paper,* No. 323. Washington, D.C.: The World Bank, 1979.

10. Carr, J., Marascuilo, L., & Serlin, R. *A measure of association for ranked tests based on the Kruskal-Wallis model.* Manuscript submitted for publication, 1979.

References

Anastasiow, N. J. John Dewey and current cognitive psychology of learning. In S. J. Meisels (Ed.), *Special education and development.* Baltimore: University Park Press, 1979.

Arthur, G. *The Arthur Adaptation of the Leiter International Performance Scale.* Beverly Hills, Ca.: Psychological Service Center Press, 1952.

Bachman, J. G., O'Malley, P. M., & Johnston, J. *Adolescence to adulthood: Change and stability in the lives of young men* (Youth in transition, Vol. VI). Ann Arbor: University of Michigan Institute for Social Research, 1978.

Baratz, S. S., & Baratz, J. C. Early childhood intervention: The social science base of institutional racism. *Harvard Educational Review,* Reprint Series No. 5, 1971, 111-132.

Becker, H. S. *Outsiders.* New York: Free Press, 1963.

Bereiter, C., & Engelmann, S. *Teaching disadvantaged children in preschool.* Englewood Cliffs, N.J.: Prentice-Hall, 1966.

Binet, A., & Simon, T. *The development of intelligence in children.* (E. S. Kite, trans.). Baltimore: Williams & Wilkins, 1916.

Blalock, H. M. *Causal inferences in non-experimental research.* Chapel Hill: University of North Carolina Press, 1961.

Bloom, B. S. *Stability and change in human characteristics.* New York: John Wiley, 1964.

Bowles, S., & Gintis, H. *Schooling in capitalist America.* New York: Basic Books, 1976.

Bronfenbrenner, U. *A report on longitudinal programs,* (Vol. II): Is early intervention effective? DHEW Publication Number (OHD) 74-24, 1974.

Bureau of Labor Statistics, *Handbook of labor statistics.* Washington, D.C.: U.S. Government Printing Office, 1978.

Campbell, D. T., & Erlebacher, A. How regression artifacts in quasi-experimental evaluations can mistakenly make compensatory education look harmful. In E. L. Struening & M. Guttentag (Eds.), *Handbook of evaluation research,* (Vol. 1). Beverly Hills: Sage Publications, 1975.

Campbell, D. T., & Stanley, J. S. Experimental and quasi-experimental designs for research on teaching. In N. L. Gage (Ed.), *Handbook of research on teaching.* Chicago: Rand McNally, 1963.

Cazden, C. B., Baratz, J. C., Labov, W., & Palmer, F. H. Language development in day care programs. In J. L. Frost (Ed.), *Revisiting early childhood education.* New York: Holt, Rinehart and Winston, 1973.

Cernkovich, S. A., & Giordano, P. C. A comparative analysis of male and female delinquency. *The Sociological Quarterly, 20,* Winter 1979, 131-145.

Cloward, R. A., & Ohlin, L. E. *Delinquency and opportunity.* Glencoe, Ill.: Free Press, 1960.

Coleman, J. S. ,Campbell, E. Q., Hobson, C. J., McPartland, J., Mood, A. M., Weinfeld, F. D., & York, R. L. *Equality of educational opportunity.* Washington, D.C.: U.S. Government Printing Office, 1966.

Collins, R. *The credential society: An historical sociology of education and stratification.* New York: Academic Press, 1979.

Conger, J. J., & Miller, W. C. *Personality, social class, and delinquency.* New York: John Wiley, 1966.

Consortium on Developmental Continuity. *The persistence of preschool effects* (Final report of grant 18-76-007843, Administration for Children, Youth, and Families, OHDS, DHEW). Washington, D.C.: ACYF, 1977.

Consortium for Longitudinal Studies. *Lasting effects after preschool* (Final report of HEW grant 90C-1311). Denver: Education Commission of the States, 1978.

Consortium for Longitudinal Studies. Lasting effects of early education. *Monographs of the Society for Research in Child Development,* 1980 (in press).

Council of Economic Advisers. *Economic indicators,* December 1979.

Cronbach, L. J. Heredity, environment, and social policy. *Harvard Educational Review, 39,* 1969, 338-347.

Cronbach, L. J., Gleser, G. C., Nanda, H., & Rajaratnam, N. *The dependability of behavioral measurements: Theory of generalizability for scores and profiles.* New York: John Wiley & Sons, 1972.

deLone, R. H. *Small futures: Inequality, children, and the failure of liberal reform.* New York: Harcourt, Brace, Jovanovich, 1978.

Deutsch, M. *An evaluation of the effectiveness of an enriched curriculum in overcoming the consequences of environmental deprivation* (Final report, project no. 5-0342, grant no. OE-5-10-045). Office of Education (DHEW), Bureau of Research, June 1, 1971.

Dunn, L. M. *Peabody Picture Vocabulary Test Manual.* Minneapolis, Minnesota: American Guidance Service, 1965.

Edmonds, R. Effective schools for the urban poor. *Educational Leadership,* October 1979, 15-24.

102

Elkind, D. Preschool education: enrichment or instruction? *Childhood Education*, 1969, *46*, 321-328.

Elliott, D. S., Ageton, S. S., & Canter, R. J. An integrated theoretical perspective on delinquent behavior. *Journal of Research in Crime and Delinquency*, January 1979.

Elliott, D. S., & Voss, H. L. *Delinquency and dropout*. Lexington, Massachusetts: Lexington Books, 1974.

Empey, L. Lubeck, S. G., & LaPorte, R. L. *Explaining delinquency: construction, test, and reformulation of a sociological theory*. Lexington, Massachusetts: Heath Lexington Books, 1971.

Epstein, A. S., & Weikart, D. P. The longitudinal follow-up of the Ypsilanti-Carnegie Infant Education Project, *Monographs of the High/Scope Educational Research Foundation*, 1979, No. 6.

Fauntleroy, J. (Ed.). *Federal education grants directory*. Washington, D.C.: Capitol Publications, 1979.

Feinberg, W. *Reason and rhetoric: The intellectual foundations of twentieth century liberal educational policy*. New York: John Wiley & Sons, 1975.

Field, T. M., Widmayer, S. M., Stringer, S., & Ignatoff, E. Teenage, lower class, black mothers and their preterm infants: An intervention and developmental follow-up. *Child Development*, *51*(2), 1980, 426-436.

Gold, M. Scholastic experiences, self-esteem, and delinquent behavior: A theory for alternative schools. *Crime and Delinquency*, July 1978, 270-328.

Gordon, I. J. International Year of the Child: Seek continuity in social policy concerning child achievement. *Young Children*, 34 (3), March 1979.

Grossman, H. (Ed.). *Manual on terminology and classification in mental retardation* (3rd ed.). Washington D.C.: American Association on Mental Deficiency, 1973.

Hargreaves, D. H. *Social relations in a secondary school*. London: Routledge and Kegan Paul, 1967.

Hawkridge, D., Chalupsky, A., & Roberts, A. *A study of selected exemplary programs for the education of disadvantaged children*. Palo Alto, California: American Institute for Research in the Behavioral Sciences, 1968.

Heise, D. R. *Causal analysis*. New York: John Wiley, 1975.

Hill, C. R., & Stafford, F. Allocation of time to preschool children and educational opportunity. *Journal of Human Resources*, 1974, *9*, 323-341.

Hirschi, T. *Causes of delinquency*. Berkeley: University of California Press, 1967.

Hirschi, T., & Hindelang, M. J. Intelligence and delinquency: A revisionist review. *American Sociological Review*, 1977, *42*, 571-587.

Hohmann, M., Banet, B., & Weikart, D. P. *Young children in action: A manual for preschool educators*. Ypsilanti, Michigan: High/Scope Press, 1979.

Hughes, J. F., & Hughes, A. O. *Equal education: A new national strategy*. Bloomington: Indiana University Press, 1972.

Hunt, J. McV. Has compensatory education failed? Has it been tried? Environment, heredity, and intelligence. *Harvard Educational Review*, Reprint Series No. 2, 1969, 130-152.

Hunt, J. McV. *Intelligence and experience*. New York: Ronald Press, 1961.

Interagency Committee for the International Year of the Child. *Report on federal government programs that relate to children*. Washington, D.C.: U.S. Department of Health, Education, and Welfare, 1979.

Jackson, P. *Life in classrooms*. New York: Holt, Rinehart, and Winston, 1968.

Jencks, C., Bartlett, S., Corcoran, M., Crouse, J., Eaglesfield, D., Jackson, G., McClelland, K., Mueser, P., Olneck, M., Schwartz, J., Ward, S., & Williams, J. *Who gets ahead? The determinants of economic success in America*. New York: Basic Books, 1979.

Jencks, C., Smith, M., Acland, H., Bane, M. J., Cohen, D., Gintis, H., Heyns, B., & Michelson, S. *Inequality: A reassessment of the effect of family and schooling in America*. New York: Basic Books, 1972.

Jensen, A. R. *Bias in mental testing*. New York: Free Press, 1980.

Jensen, A. R. How much can we boost IQ and scholastic achievement? *Harvard Educational Review*, 1969, *39*, 1-123.

Jensen, G. F. Race, achievement, and delinquency: A further look at *Delinquency in a birth cohort*. *American Journal of Sociology*, 1976, *82* (2), 379-387.

Karier, C. *Shaping the American educational state: 1900 to the present*. New York: Free Press, 1975.

Katz, M. B. *The irony of early school reform: Educational innovation in mid-nineteenth century Massachusetts*. Boston: Beacon Press, 1968.

Keniston, K. *All our children: The American family under pressure*. New York: Harcourt, Brace, Jovanovich, 1977.

Klaus, R., & Gray, S. W. The early training project for disadvantaged children: A report after five years. *Monographs of the Society for Research in Child Development*, *33*(4, Serial No. 120), 1968.

Lewis, O. *Five familes: Mexican case studies in the culture of poverty.* New York: Basic Books, 1959.

McCarthy, J. J., & Kirk, S. A. *Examiner's manual: Illinois Test of Psycholinguistic Abilities, experimental version.* Urbana: University of Illinois, Institute for Research on Exceptional Children, 1961.

Occupational Characteristics. Washington, D.C.: U.S. Government Printing Office, 1973. [PC [2]—7A]

Ogbu, J. U. *Minority education and caste: The American system in cross-cultural perspective.* New York: Academic Press, 1978.

Perspectives on the Follow Through evaluation. *Harvard Educational Review, 48*(2), 1978, 125-192.

Piaget, J. *The psychology of intelligence* (M. Piercy & D. E. Berlyne, trans.). Totowa, New Jersey: Littlefield, Adams, & Co., 1966.

Polk, K., & Shafer, W. E. *Schools and delinquency.* Englewood Cliffs, New Jersey: Prentice-Hall, 1972.

Rainwater, L. Neutralizing the disinherited: Some psychological aspects of understanding the poor. In V. L. Allen (Ed.), *Psychological factors in poverty.* Chicago: Markham Publishing Company, 1970.

Ravitch, D. *The revisionists revised: A critique of the radical attack on the schools.* New York: Basic Books, 1977.

Rehberg, R. A., & Rosenthal, E. R. *Class and merit in the American high school.* New York: Longman, 1978.

Rhodes, A. L., & Reiss, A. J. Apathy, truancy, and delinquency as adaptions to school failure, *Social Forces, 1969, 48,* 12-22.

Rist, R. C. Student social class and teacher expectations: The self-fulfilling prophecy in ghetto education. *Harvard Educational Review,* Reprint Series, No. 5, 1971, 70-110.

Rosenthal, R., & Jacobson, L. *Pygmalion in the classroom: Teacher expectation and pupils' intellectual development.* New York: Holt, Rinehart, and Winston, 1968.

Royster, E. C., & Larson, J. C. *Executive summary of a national survey of Head Start graduates and their peers.* Cambridge, Massachusetts: Abt Associates, 1978.

Ruopp, R. Travers, J., Glantz, F., & Coelen, C. *Children at the center: Summary findings and their implications* (Vol. 1, Final report of the National Day Care Study). Cambridge, Massachusetts: Abt Associates, 1979.

Schaefer, E. S., & Bell, R. Q. Development of a parental attitude research instrument. *Child Development,* 1958, *28,* 339-361.

Schafer, W. E., & Olexa, C. *Tracking and opportunity: The locking out process and beyond.* Scranton, Pa: Chandler Publications, 1971.

Sellin, T., & Wolfgang, M. E. *The measurement of delinquency.* New York: John Wiley and Sons, 1964.

Silverberg, N. E., & Silverberg, M. C. School achievement and delinquency. *Review of Educational Research, 1971, 41* (1), 17-33.

Skeels, H. M. Adult status of children with contrasting early life experiences. *Monographs of the Society for Research in Child Development,* 1966, *31,* (3, Serial No. 105).

Skeels, H. M., & Dye, H. G. A study of the effects of differential stimulation on mentally retarded children. *Proceedings of the American Association on Mental Deficiency, 1939, 44,* 114-136.

Snow, R. E. Unfinished Pygmalion. *Contemporary Psychology, 1969, 14,* 197-199.

Terman, L. M., & Merrill, M. A. *Stanford-Binet Intelligence Scale Form L-M: Manual for the third revision.* Boston: Houghton-Mifflin, 1960.

Thorndike, R. L., Review of R. Rosenthal & L. Jacobson, *Pygmalion in the classroom. American Educational Research Journal,* 1968, *5,* 708-711.

Tiegs, E. W., & Clark, W. W. *Manual: California Achievement Test, complete battery.* Monterey Park: California Test Bureau (McGraw-Hill), 1963.

Tiegs, E. W., & Clark, W. W. *Test coordinator's handbook: California Achievement Tests.* Monterey, California: California Test Bureau (McGraw-Hill), 1970.

Turner, R. *The social context of ambition.* San Francisco: Chandler, 1964.

Valentine, C. A. *Culture and poverty: Critique and counter-proposals.* Chicago: University of Chicago Press, 1968.

Valentine, C. A., & Valentine, B. L. Making the scene, digging the action, and telling it like it is: Anthropologists at work in a dark ghetto. In N. Whitten & J. Szwed (Eds.), *Afro-American anthropology: Contemporary perspectives.* New York: Free Press, 1969.

Vinter, R. D., Sarri, R. S., Vorwaller, D. J., & Schafer, W. E. *Pupil Behavior Inventory: A manual of administration and scoring.* Ann Arbor: Campus Publishers, 1966.

Weber, C. U., Foster, P. W., & Weikart, D. P. An economic analysis of the Ypsilanti Perry Preschool Project. *Monographs of the High/Scope Educational Research Foundation,* 1978, No. 4.

Wechsler, D. *Manual for the Wechsler Intelligence Scale for Children (revised)*. New York: The Psychological Corporation, 1974.

Weikart, D. P. (Ed.) *Preschool intervention: Preliminary results of the Perry Preschool Project*. Ann Arbor: Campus Publishers, 1967.

Weikart, D. P., Bond, J. T., & McNeil, J. T. The Ypsilanti Perry Preschool Project: Preschool years and longitudinal results through fourth grade. *Monographs of the High/Scope Educational Research Foundation,* 1978, No. 3.

Weikart, D. P., Deloria, D., Lawser, S., & Wiegerink, R. Longitudinal results of the Ypsilanti Perry Preschool Project. *Monographs of the High/Scope Educational Research Foundation,* 1970, No. 1.

Weikart, D. P., Epstein, A. S., Schweinhart, L. J., & Bond, J. T. The Ypsilanti Preschool Curriculum Demonstration Project: Preschool years and longitudinal results. *Monographs of the High/Scope Educational Research Foundation,* 1978, No. 4.

Weikart, D. P., Rogers, L., Adcock, C., & McClelland, D. *The Cognitively Oriented Curriculum: A framework for preschool teachers.* Urbana: University of Illinois—NAEYC, 1971.

Westinghouse Learning Corporation & Ohio University. *The impact of Head Start experience on children's cognitive and affective development.* Springfield, Virginia: U. S. Department of Commerce Clearinghouse, 1969. (PB 184 328)

White, S., Day, M. C., Freeman, P. K., Hantman, S. A., & Messenger K. P. *Federal programs for young children: Review and recommendations* Washington, D. C.: U. S. Government Printing Office, 1973.(Publication No. (OS) 74-101.)

Wolfgang, M. E., Figlio, R. M, & Sellin, T. *Delinquency in a birth cohort.* Chicago: University of Chicago Press, 1972.

Wylie, R. *The self-concept, Volume 1: A review of methodological considerations and measuring instruments* (revised ed.). Lincoln: University of Nebraska Press, 1974.

Zigler, E., & Butterfield, E. C. Motivational aspects of changes in IQ test performance of culturally deprived nursery school children. *Child Development,* 1968, 39 (1), 1-14.

Zigler, E., & Valentine, J. (Eds.) *Project Head Start: A legacy of the War on Poverty.* New York: The Free Press, 1979.

COMMENTARY BY ASA HILLIARD
Callaway Professor of Urban Education
Georgia State University

High/Scope's Perry Preschool Project has been a bold and courageous effort. Longitudinal studies do not represent the easy way out for educational researchers. Longitudinal studies which utilize experimental and control groups with subjects assigned on a random basis are indeed rare. Even more rare are the researchers who go beyond observations and conduct intervention programs which are designed to improve the lot of children for whom educational forecasts have been gloomy. In a way, those who do such studies place their professional reputations on the line, for outside observers will look not only at what the children do, but will examine the intervention for its validity and wisdom as well. In the face of the probability of close professional scrutiny and in the face of certain phenomenal logistical difficulties which are associated with any longitudinal research effort, a group which embarks upon such a venture is certainly entitled to respect and gratitude from those among our ranks who have initiated much more modest efforts.

The Perry Preschool Project was initiated during the early 60's. Such a project if initiated today might very well appear quite ordinary. However, during the early 60's, the Perry Preschool Project was anything but ordinary, not only because of its initiation as a longitudinal experimental study, but because it challenged a widespread prevailing wisdom: either that poor children did not have the capacity to learn, or that the effects of poverty were so overwhelming that there could be little hope for breaking its cycle. Certainly then as now, no one would expect that preschool experiences alone would be able to provide children with resources for overcoming the terrible effects of poverty and racism in any total way. However, there are those who believe that significant improvements can be made in the lives of children prior to the time that wholesale changes take place within the society.

Readers of this monograph will find two kinds of language: On the one hand, there is a language which is the legacy of the 1960's. For example, the 60's was an era in which educators talked about many Black children as being "culturally deprived," "economically deprived," and "cognitively deprived." Sometimes the lable "disadvantaged" was used instead of "deprived." In either case, the image which was called forth when thinking about poor Black children was that they were somehow vessels that were only partially filled, vessels which could be compared to more "normal" middle-class vessels which were completely full. The idea that fully intelligent behavior could find expression in an environment quite different from that to which most White middle-class Americans were exposed, was quite foreign to many educational researchers. Children were thought to be deficient rather than different. So, for example, when this monograph refers to the improvement of "cognitive ability," it uses language which is a legacy of an earlier era. Certainly, the schools will require that children use a particular language and a particular set of skills. The acquisition of such language and skills requires cognitive ability. However, cognitive ability also exists in non-school environments. Children in non-school environments, in poverty communities organize their experiences, categorize, classify, reason and do problem-solving. The distinction is a matter of content and not mental process.

Happily, this monograph speaks a second language. That second language represents an evolution from the first which takes into account some of the better thinking and more enlightened perspectives on poor and cultural minority children and their relationship to the wider society. The concept of a transactional approach recognizes clearly the contribution that both the child and care-givers make toward child outcomes. In orientation, the Perry Preschool Project is right to seek a balance between the "internal self-originated motivations, attitudes and abilities against external indicators of expectation, approval, or disapproval." The concept of social psychological bonding, which incorporates the child's school achievement, the child's commitment to schooling, and the social reinforcement which the child receives as part of the school experience is a potentially fruitful paradigm. In looking at the strength of bonds, it becomes necessary to look at the behavior of children and their care-givers simultaneously.

The Perry Preschool Project relies upon a dimension which has been described as "cognitive stimulation" by preschool education. In looking at what has been done with the children, it becomes extremely important to distinguish between "cognitive stimulation" and the training of children in particular content. In other words, is it the case that interventions make children's mental operations grow, or is what we see simply a matter that they have applied their cognitive powers to new content—specifically to school content? Although the intervention will be quite possibly the same, no matter which of these two beliefs is held by teachers, it becomes extremely important to articulate which of the two beliefs is held. If it is believed that a child cannot think, does not reason, is in some way "underdeveloped mentally," then in addition to professional interventions to improve cognitive functioning, there will be feelings about the child by those who are designated to help the child. Helpers may feel anything from sympathy to revulsion. Clearly, present school practices indicate low status for remedial programs and high status for programs which are designed to serve bright or gifted children. If, on the other hand, it is recognized that new information and skills are being taught to children who have not had the opportunity to learn them, even though they may possess rich information and skills in another context, then those who intervene can work with such children without regarding them as pathetic objects of professional attention.

Having had the opportunity to see some of the High/Scope Foundation's interventions in operation, I found myself being very impressed with the educational climate that has produced such excellent results for more than a decade. The data show significant differences between the experimental and control groups in the Perry Preschool Project. The experimental group had initially higher IQ's, stronger commitment to schooling, were rated higher in motivation for school, had higher school achievement, were referred less frequently for special education, and were rated as better developed socially and as having higher aspirations for children by parents. Preschoolers were found to be less deviant in their school behavior. When preschool children become adolescents, they tended to have a higher rate of employment than non-preschoolers.

Therefore, on the above as well as several other variables, preschool seemed to make a positive difference for children both in the short run and in the long run. Even though the findings in favor of preschool are sometimes small, when all the findings are taken together, one cannot help but be impressed with their consistency in the general direction of benefits for preschool children.

The interpretation of the findings tends to place significant weight on the value of the cognitively oriented curriculum in preschool. This is certainly understandable when looking at such criteria as IQ test scores or achievement test scores. However, it would be pushing things a great deal to attribute certain outcomes directly to preschool or to the nature of the preschool experience. Undoubtedly, the institution of a cognitively oriented curriculum or any structured preschool program which is carried out over a long period of time will operate to mobilize a variety of resources within a small social system. One can speculate that the behavior of parents towards young children will be quite different when their young child is given close attention in preschool, and that behavior may also be quite different as a consequence of success experiences with schools during the child's younger years. We may speculate that parents could become less awed with the school as an institution, more trusting and more familiar with mechanisms for getting things done. In general, one might speculate that the initiation of the preschool project with its several facets actually brought into play many more forces than those which were originally planned.

Undoubtedly, there will be those who will nit-pick statistics or experimental-design procedures. However, the general direction of the findings in this study shows clear, positive results in favor of preschool experiences for children. On the whole, these findings are both scientifically sound and intuitively valid. The Perry Preschool Project has some things in common with recent research which shows that the amount of time which teachers and students spend in a focused teaching/learning situation is directly related to outcomes for children. We hear this called "time on task." The Perry Preschool Project represents "time on *several* tasks" with results which might be expected, based upon what we know from other time-on-task studies.

This monograph will stand as one of a kind. All the findings are important. The Perry Preschool Project establishes an excellent model for approaching both intervention and evaluation activity. Overall, the positive results of this study far outweigh its minimal limitations. The Perry Preschool Project will stand as one of the more important studies of its time, and is now a kind of standard against which other efforts in intervention and evaluation must be compared.

ASA HILLIARD
GEORGIA STATE UNIVERSITY

COMMENTARY BY PAUL N. YLVISAKER
Dean, Graduate School of Education
Harvard University

Weikart and colleagues have tenaciously drawn an optimistic trend line through the jagged crests of euphoria and the plunging canyons of pessimism that were the flowing landscape of American social and educational thought through the Sixties and Seventies. In a carefully-documented experiment, they've demonstrated that poor black kids with low recorded IQs can respond to early intervention

—by doing significantly better in their later schooling,

—by toning down the more serious anti-social behavior they predictably might otherwise have engaged in,

—by justifying in straight-dollar terms the additional social outlays invested in their preschooling.

No matter that their recorded IQs rose only momentarily; they, and our society, are the better for the opportunity they were given.

One should add, with scholarly caution, the words "so far." The experimental and control groups have been trailed in this volume only through early adolescence. Critical life stages and an ominous global voyage lie ahead. But a better beginning has been made. And that's good news enough for educators whom critics have left wondering whether anything at all could be done to give impoverished minority children a fairer start.

As a shot-in-the-arm, I would couple this happy outcome with the studied optimism emerging from the research of Michael Rudder and Peter Mortimore in London and of Ronald Edmonds and others in the United States. They, too, have had the good sense to ask an essential question and the perseverence to sift through accumulating experience and data to find the essential answer. That essential question is whether schooling can make a difference in the life of a disadvantaged child. The essential answer seems to be that it can—provided there is enough commitment to make it so.

That message of commitment comes through even more explicitly in the studies of effective schools than it does in the Perry Preschool evaluation. The reason may be obvious: Edmonds et al. began their inquiries with schools that "worked"; student performance was known to be superior. What remained to be identified were the characteristics that made those schools effective. Weikart and his colleagues started their own preschool, then focussed their assessment on behavioral patterns of pupils which would indicate success or failure. Whether because of modesty or an understandable passion for objectivity, there is little in this monograph that enables one to get the feel of the learning environment they created—or of the school system into which they delivered their preschoolers. More of this qualitative dimension appears in a preceding volume (Weikart, Bond, and McNeil, 1978). Still, one can easily sense the personal commitment that nurtured this enterprise—at least the preschool phase of it. The fact and importance of that commitment keeps shining through, even when abstracted into the theoretical formulations with which the authors begin and conclude their account of why early schooling can succeed: viz., early exposure to a more stimulating (read also supportive) learning environment induces greater self-confidence and progressively greater success in meeting the school's norms of achievement and behavior. True, that could mean simply that preschoolers acquire a facility for manipulating the system earlier on, but this more cynical interpretation does not seem to square with the idealistic values which Weikart and his co-workers profess, nor with the dedication which kept them at it over such a long and arduous period.

Both as an analyst and as an activist I would have liked to have seen more attention given to those human and environmental qualities that must have helped this experiment succeed. Admittedly, it is easier to say that now when the literature is moving in this direction. Over the years of their involvement, Weikart and his associates were understandably preoccupied with growing numbers of skeptics seeking proof by the numbers. Words like "commitment" and concepts like "ethos" became unfashionable carryovers from the rhetoric of social reform. To have relied upon, or even addressed, them too explicitly might have seemed to weaken the case.

Thankfully, commitment was there. It produced an act of faith that seems to have paid off, and an extended assessment which proves again the extraordinary value of longitudinal research. That can be said even if the performance of the experimental group had not been, or might later turn out not to be, demonstrably better. Not enough of such research is being done—due partly to the short life of funding tastes and availability, and equally, if not more so, to the staccato style of research careers and perceived rewards. I wonder if it would help if private philanthropy (it seems too much to ask of government) were to adopt a policy that at least some fraction of their experimental projects be structured so as to ensure a continuing assessment. In that perspective, one has to applaud the efforts of the Consortium for Longitudinal Studies referred to so frequently in the monograph. The Consortium, against the odds, is moving in the right direction.

Still the most powerful message of this solidly-researched venture is for the educators of the 1980's and 1990's to take heart—and let's pray they take heed. During those years, our cities and our schools will be filling with minorities: youthful newcomers to American society and their youngsters, mostly poor, mostly having to play catch-up learning, mostly seen by the resident majority as threats or liabilities. The sad legacy we carry from the depressing '70's is the discouragement that echoes from those short-range and short-sighted studies that in effect said to educators, "you might as well not even try." But try we must if we are not to wipe out those millions of newcomers and the social potential— more than that, the social necessity—they represent. Because the truth is, this nation's defense, its work force, its cultural and social rejuvenation will all be wanting if these newcoming minorities are wasted.

The commitment shown by the Ypsilanti Perry Preschool group wins my thanks and respect.

PAUL N. YLVISAKER
HARVARD UNIVERSITY